Plays About Our Nation's Songs

Royalty-free plays, pageants, and programs dramatizing in songs and scenes the story of America growing

By

AILEEN FISHER

Publishers   PLAYS, INC.   *Boston*

C O N T E N T S

PLAYS ABOUT OUR NATION'S SONGS

Sing, America, Sing

Characters

(Many parts may be doubled up)

NARRATOR

GIRLS CHORUS

STAGEHAND

TWO WOMEN

SONS OF LIBERTY

RAGGED CONTINENTALS

FRANCIS SCOTT KEY

JOHN SKINNER

SAILORS

LUMBERJACKS

MULE DRIVER

COTTON PICKERS

TWO RAILWAY WORKERS

UNION SOLDIERS

CONFEDERATE SOLDIERS

DANIEL, JAMIE *and* REBECCA BOONE

PIONEERS

COWBOYS

WORLD WAR SOLDIERS

RADIO VOICE

Note: Words and music for the well-known songs in this play may be obtained from many different song books. The less familiar songs marked with an asterisk (*) may be found in *A Treasury of American Song*, by Downes and Siegmeister, published by Alfred A. Knopf, New York.

SETTING: *Large, bare stage.*

AT RISE: NARRATOR *stands at one side.* GIRLS CHORUS, *which will be on stage throughout the play, stands or sits at back. As curtain opens* CHORUS *is softly singing 1st stanza of "America the Beautiful."*

NARRATOR: Sing, America, sing! Sing of the past and the present, of peace and war. Sing of the beginnings and endings and goings-on. Sing of the days when we were thirteen colonies along the Atlantic seaboard, in a new world, facing a new horizon. Thirteen states waiting for a new flag!

CHORUS (*Speaking in turn, staccato*): New Hampshire . . . Massachusetts . . . Rhode Island . . . Connecticut . . . New York . . . New Jersey . . . Delaware . . . Pennsylvania . . . Maryland . . . Virginia . . . North Carolina . . . South Carolina . . . Georgia.

NARRATOR: Sing of a word called *liberty* beginning to stir through the colonies like a breeze off the sea, gathering strength, gathering force, sweeping along the coast . . . shipyard to crossroad, crossroad to farmhouse, farmhouse to tavern, tavern to cobblestone street.

CHORUS (*Softly at first, mounting to fortissimo*): Liberty . . . liberty . . . liberty . . . liberty . . . LIBERTY. (STAGEHAND *enters on side opposite* NARRATOR, *puts up sign reading* NEW YORK, 1769. *Exits.* TWO WOMEN *enter, talking.*)

1ST WOMAN: It's always exciting to walk past the Common and see if the Liberty Pole is still standing. (*Stops, looks, points*) Look, the banner still flaps defiance at the British soldiers.

2ND WOMAN (*Nodding*): So that is your Liberty Pole! I've heard about it, even in Boston. A sacred symbol in the struggle against tyranny. No taxation without representation!

1ST WOMAN: I should say not! We won't stand for it. Our Sons of Liberty in New York guard the Pole like bulldogs. Three times the British have cut it down. Four times the Sons of Liberty have raised it! This fourth Pole has survived for several years now.

2ND WOMAN: How could the British cut it down—with those iron bars around it, held in place by metal hoops?

1ST WOMAN: They have tried—not only to cut it down, but to undermine it and blow it up. And each time they failed.

2ND WOMAN: And if they do manage to destroy it, your Sons of Liberty will raise another. (*Cocks ear*) Listen!

1ST WOMAN (*Listening, as strains of music are heard offstage, voices singing*): "The Liberty Song!"* Everyone is singing it here . . . that is, everyone on our side.

2ND WOMAN: We sing it in Boston, too. (*They step back to join* CHORUS *as* SONS OF LIBERTY *come in singing.*)

SONS OF LIBERTY:
"Come join hand in hand, brave Americans all,
And rouse your bold hearts at fair Liberty's call;
No tyrannous acts shall suppress your just claim,
Or stain with dishonor America's name."

CHORUS (*Joins in*):
"In Freedom we're born and in Freedom we'll live,
Our purses are ready,
Steady, friends, steady;
Not as slaves, but as free men our money we'll give."
(SONS OF LIBERTY *pass hats;* CHORUS *and* WOMEN *put in coins.* SONS OF LIBERTY *sing again.*)

SONS OF LIBERTY: "Then join hand in hand, brave Americans all, (*They join with* CHORUS *and* WOMEN *and circle around stage.*)
By uniting we stand, by dividing we fall;
In so righteous a cause let us hope to succeed,
For heaven approves of each generous deed."

(They break circle, and SONS OF LIBERTY *pass hats again as they all swing into the chorus of "The Liberty Song." On last line,* SONS OF LIBERTY *march out;* CHORUS *moves back in place;* TWO WOMEN *exit.* STAGEHAND *enters, removes sign, and exits.)*

NARRATOR: Sing, America, sing of the long hard war for liberty and independence—1775 to 1783—years of suffering and hardship, doubt and faith, hope and uncertainty. Sing of courage in the face of overwhelming odds.

CHORUS (*Speaking in turn, staccato*): Lexington . . . Concord . . . Bunker Hill . . . Trenton . . . Germantown . . . Valley Forge . . . Monmouth . . . Charlestown . . . Camden . . . Yorktown.

NARRATOR: Sing of General Washington and his ragged Continentals! (CONTINENTALS *march in, singing "Yankee Doodle."*)

CONTINENTALS:
"Fath'r and I went down to camp
Along with Captain Good'in,
And there we saw the men and boys
As thick as hasty puddin'."

CHORUS (*Taking over while* CONTINENTALS *mark time.* CHORUS *might put on paper soldier caps, each with a big feather*):
"Yankee Doodle keep it up,
Yankee Doodle dandy,
Mind the music and the step
And with the girls be handy."

CONTINENTALS:
"And there was General Washington
Upon a slapping stallion,
A-giving orders to his men:
I guess there was a million."

CHORUS (*Repeats chorus, as* CONTINENTALS *maneuver and march out*):

"Yankee Doodle keep it up" . . . (*Etc.*)

NARRATOR: Sing, America, sing. Sing of the long war over and independence won. Sing of the blessings of liberty secured to ourselves and our posterity. Sing of our new nation stretching and spreading, reaching toward the west . . . up the river valleys, through the forests, over the mountains. Sing of new states coming into the Union.

CHORUS (*In turn*): Vermont . . . Kentucky . . . Tennessee . . . Ohio . . . Louisiana. (CHORUS *swings into* "*Hail, Columbia!*")

"Firm, united let us be
Rallying round our Liberty!
As a band of brothers join'd,
Peace and safety we shall find."

NARRATOR: And sing of the War of 1812 that gave Francis Scott Key the idea for our national anthem. (STAGEHAND *enters, puts up sign*: CHESAPEAKE BAY, SEPT., 1814, *exits*. FRANCIS SCOTT KEY *comes in, paces nervously, peers out, jots down note on envelope*. JOHN SKINNER *enters*.)

SKINNER: Aren't you going to rest at all, Mr. Key? You've been pacing the deck all night, back and forth, back and forth.

KEY: Not all night, Mr. Skinner. Some of the time I have stood silently staring across the Bay at Fort McHenry.

SKINNER: Watching the bombs bursting in air . . .

KEY: Yes, and the rockets' red glare. Through the flashing brightness of the bombardment, I have strained my eyes to see if our flag kept flying.

SKINNER (*Peering out*): And is it still flying?

KEY: The last I saw, yes. Fort McHenry has not surrendered. I wish I might have been there to help defend it, sir, instead of fidgeting out here in the Bay detained by the British fleet.

SKINNER: At least our rescue mission was a success. The British released the prisoner and we can take him back to Baltimore with us when the siege is lifted. Thank God the British Admiral was wrong about the bombardment, Mr. Key!

KEY: Expecting to capture Fort McHenry in a few hours! Why, they've been shelling the Fort for a day and a night and, if I'm not mistaken, our flag *still* flies over it. (*Peers out*) I wish I could see for sure. (*As* KEY *and* SKINNER *strain their eyes,* CHORUS *sings first stanza of "The Star-Spangled Banner," pantomiming as if they, too, were on deck watching anxiously.*)

CHORUS:

"Oh, say, can you see, by the dawn's early light,
What so proudly we hailed at the twilight's last gleaming?
Whose broad stripes and bright stars, through the perilous fight,
O'er the ramparts we watched, were so gallantly streaming!
And the rockets' red glare, the bombs bursting in air,
Gave proof through the night that our flag was still there;
(*Voices up*)
Oh, say, does that Star-Spangled Banner yet wave
O'er the land of the free and the home of the brave?"

SKINNER: If only we could catch the gleam of the first light of dawn on our flag, Mr. Key!

KEY (*Making note on envelope*): Catching the gleam of the morning's first beam . . .

SKINNER: You are a poet as well as a lawyer?

KEY: Oh, occasionally I am moved to write verses. All last night, while the bombs were bursting, my brain was on fire. Not just kindled, sir, but on fire . . . as I thought about our star-spangled banner waving bravely through the fight. (*Taps envelope*) I have words here, phrases here, that need only to be put together when I reach Baltimore. They will make a song, perhaps.

CHORUS (*Up suddenly, excited*):
"Now it catches the gleam of the morning's first beam,
In full glory reflected now shines on the stream;
'Tis the star-spangled banner; oh, long may it wave
O'er the land of the free and the home of the brave!"
(KEY *and* SKINNER *exit during the singing.* STAGEHAND *enters, removes sign, exits.*)

NARRATOR: Sing, America, of white stars on a field of blue, a star for every state, and every state growing, developing. Wagons creaking. Hammers pounding. Sails flapping. Axes ringing. Millstones grinding. Clipper ships sailing the seven seas. Sing of America at work, making our country great! (SAILORS *enter singing "Blow, Boys, Blow."* As they sing, they pantomime pulling on ropes to hoist sails.*)

SOLO: "A Yankee ship came down the river,"

SAILORS: "Blow, boys, blow!"

SOLO: "Her masts and yards they shone like silver."

SAILORS: "Blow, my bully boys, blow!"

SOLO: "How do you know she's a Yankee liner?"

SAILORS: "Blow, boys, blow!"

SOLO: "The Stars and Stripes float out behind her."

SAILORS: "Blow, my bully boys, blow!" (*One of the* SAILORS *might go into a hornpipe here. Or the* CHORUS *might do a sailor dance if that seems more practicable. Then* SAILORS *take up their song again.*)

SOLO: "Blow, boys, blow, the sun's drawing water."

SAILORS: "Blow, boys, blow!"

SOLO: "Three cheers for the cook and one for his daughter."

SAILORS (*As they go out*): "Blow, my bully boys, blow!"

NARRATOR: Sing of the lumberjack cutting down the white pines in New England forests . . . trimming a tall straight mast . . . sawing logs for timbers and building-boards . . . riding the logs down the river on the spring flood. (*Several* LUMBERJACKS *enter. They swing axes in pantomime as they sing "A Shantyman's Life"**)

LUMBERJACKS:

"Oh a shantyman's life is a wearisome life
Although some think it void of care.
Swinging an axe from morning till night,
In the midst of the forests so drear.
Lying in the shanty—bleak and cold
While the cold, stormy wintery winds blow,
And as soon as the daylight doth appear,
To the wild woods we must go." (LUMBERJACKS *repeat last two lines as they go out.*)

NARRATOR: Sing of the mule-drivers guiding boats and barges along the Erie Canal, night and day, day and night—moving passengers and produce and drawing the country together. (MULE DRIVER *enters, pantomiming driving his mule, singing "The Erie Canal."**)

MULE DRIVER: "I've got a mule and her name is Sal,"

CHORUS: "Fifteen miles on the Erie Canal—"

MULE DRIVER: "She's a good old worker and a good old pal,"

CHORUS: "Fifteen miles on the Erie Canal."

MULE DRIVER:

"We've hauled some barges in our day,
Filled with lumber, coal and hay,
And we know every inch of the way
From Albany to Buffalo."

CHORUS *and* DRIVER:

"Low bridge, everybody down! (CHORUS *ducks down*).
For it's Low Bridge, we're coming to a town! (*Down again*)
You can always tell your neighbor,
You can always tell your pal,
If you've ever navigated on the Erie Canal." (MULE DRIVER *and* CHORUS *may sing another stanza, "We'd bet-*

ter get along on our way, old gal," etc., with chorus if desired. MULE DRIVER *goes out at end of chorus.*)

NARRATOR: Sing of the blacksmith, the miller, the farmer, the storekeeper, the fisherman, the baker, the candlestick maker. Sing of the miner, the tavern keeper, the peddler trekking down the road with a pack on his back. Sing of all the men and women building America, making it strong. And sing in a minor key of the cotton pickers in the South . . . in the days when one human being could own another. (*Three or four girls,* COTTON PICKERS, *come in with sacks in which they pantomime putting cotton as they pick it. They sing "Nobody Knows de Trouble I See."*)

COTTON PICKERS:

"Nobody knows de trouble I see,
Nobody knows but Jesus;
Nobody knows de trouble I see,
Glory hallelujah!"

SOLO: "Sometimes I'm up, sometimes I'm down,"

ALL: "Oh, yes, Lord;"

SOLO: "Sometimes I'm almost to de groun',"

ALL: "Oh, yes, Lord." (*They move offstage slowly, humming as they pick cotton.*)

NARRATOR: Sing of the husky immigrants working on the railroads, pushing the gleaming rails across the prairies, through the heart of America, into the mountains. (*Two* RAILWAY WORKERS *enter. They pantomime driving spikes, taking turns hitting the spike with a sledge hammer. They sing "Pat Works on the Railway."**)

1ST WORKER:

"In eighteen hundred and forty-one
I put me corduroy britches on,
I put me corduroy britches on
To work upon the railway."

BOTH: "Fi-li-me-oo-re-oo-re-ay" . . . (*Etc.*)

2ND WORKER:

"It's Pat, do this, and Pat, do that!
Without a stocking or a hat,
And nothing but an old cravat,
While Pat works on the railway."

BOTH: "Fi-li-me-oo-re-oo-re-ay" . . . (*Etc.*)

(RAILWAY WORKERS *exit as* CHORUS *sings "She'll Be Comin' Round the Mountain." They shade their eyes, look offstage expectantly, nod at each other, look again.*)

CHORUS: "She'll be comin' round the mountain when she comes . . ." (*Etc.*) (*If possible the toot of a train whistle should be heard offstage as the song ends.*)

NARRATOR: Sing of America continuing to grow and stretch. Sixteen new white stars added to the field of blue between the War of 1812 and the War Between the States! Sixteen new shining stars.

CHORUS (*Speaking in turn, staccato*): Indiana . . . Mississippi . . . Illinois . . . Alabama . . . Maine . . . Missouri . . . Arkansas . . . Michigan . . . Florida . . . Texas . . . Iowa . . . Wisconsin . . . California . . . Minnesota . . . Oregon . . . Kansas.

NARRATOR: And then came the War Between the States, on the heels of the great debates over slavery.

1ST IN CHORUS: Abraham Lincoln has been saying for years that this country cannot endure half slave and half free.

2ND: Stephen A. Douglas doesn't agree with him.

3RD: Nobody wants war, but sometimes there seems to be no other way out.

4TH: Lincoln's idea of democracy is that we should be neither slaves nor masters.

5TH: They say in the South that slavery is good for both the whites and the blacks.

6TH: Who says it? Not the blacks!

NARRATOR: Union soldiers were on the march after the attack on Fort Sumter, and in time "The Battle Hymn

of the Republic" became their marching song. (CHORUS
sings first stanza of "The Battle Hymn of the Republic"
as UNION SOLDIERS *march in and drill on left of stage*.)
And here come Confederate soldiers on the march, to
the tune of "Dixie." (CHORUS *sings chorus of "Dixie" as*
CONFEDERATE SOLDIERS *march in and stand at right*.) And
sing of the two forces together, Union and Confederate,
both weary for home, wanting the war to stop, dreaming
the same dreams, singing the same song . . . (UNION
and CONFEDERATE SOLDIERS *move around as if setting up
camp, singing "Tenting Tonight."**)

SOLDIERS (*Softly*):
    "We're tenting tonight on the old camp ground,
    Give us a song to cheer
    Our weary hearts, a song of home
    And friends we love so dear."

SOLO UNION SOLDIER:
    "Many are the hearts that are weary tonight,
    Wishing for the war to cease;"

SOLO CONFEDERATE SOLDIER:
    "Many are the hearts that are looking for the right.
    To see the dawn of peace."

SOLDIERS:
    "Tenting tonight, tenting tonight,
    Tenting on the old camp ground."

NARRATOR: Sing of the war over and the Union safe. The
    re-united States of America! Sing of soldiers marching
    not to battle, but home again to the farms and towns of
    the North and South, to the loved ones left behind. Sing,
    America, sing! (CHORUS *joyously sings "When Johnny
    Comes Marching Home,"** *as* SOLDIERS *begin to march,
    some offstage, some changing places. This should be a
    very lively scene*.)

CHORUS:
    "When Johnny comes marching home again,"

SOLDIERS: "Hurrah! Hurrah!"

CHORUS: "We'll give him a hearty welcome then,"

SOLDIERS: "Hurrah! Hurrah!"

CHORUS: "The men will cheer, the boys will shout" . . . (*Etc.*) (CHORUS *goes into second stanza,* "*The old church bell will peal with joy,*" *and* SOLDIERS *again take the* "*Hurrahs!*" *During chorus,* SOLDIERS *begin to leave stage.*)

NARRATOR: Sing, America—sing of the pioneers forever searching for the promised land. Sing of the fearless, self-reliant men and women who kept pushing the frontier farther and farther west . . . building their cabins, tilling their piece of good earth, helping to make our country big and broad, beginning even before the Revolution. (CHORUS *might put on sunbonnets for this section. They keep swinging into the refrain from* "*The Promised Land*"* *as a sort of undertone for the scene.*)

CHORUS:

"I am bound for the promised land,
I'm bound for the promised land,
Oh, who will come and go with me?
I am bound for the promised land."

NARRATOR: Sing of pioneers pressing westward on foot, on horseback, in covered wagon . . . taming the wilderness, turning prairies into cornfields. Sing of Daniel Boone and the thousands and hundreds of thousands who came after him, lured by the adventure of pushing our frontiers westward. (STAGEHAND *enters and puts out placard*—BOONE'S FARM, NORTH CAROLINA, 1769. *He exits.* DANIEL BOONE *and son,* JAMIE, *enter.*)

JAMIE: What's beyond the hills, Pappy?

DANIEL: Sights. Wondrous sights.

JAMIE: What's beyond the mountains?

DANIEL: More sights. (*Points*) Beyond this state there's

Tennessee and Kentucky-land. Wilderness country. Like paradise, Jamie.

JAMIE: Heard you talking to that Finley man yesterday, Pappy. (REBECCA BOONE *comes in behind them, stands listening.*)

DANIEL: He's off to explore Kentucky, Finley is. And I've an itching in my feet to go along. If it weren't for your mother, now, and the younger children . . .

REBECCA: You don't have to be worryin' about us, Dan'l. (DANIEL *and* JAMIE *turn with a start.*) Weather's good, now spring is here. We'll be all right this summer. Might be you could find us a good home site in Kentucky.

DANIEL (*Excited*): It sounds like the promised land to me, Rebecca. Wouldn't be a-tall surprised if I could find the best home site we ever laid eyes on! (*As they go out,* CHORUS *sings, "I am bound for the promised land," etc.* STAGEHAND *enters, removes sign, exits.*)

NARRATOR: Sing of thousands and hundreds of thousands fired by the spirit of Daniel Boone. (TWO WOMEN *enter.*)

1ST WOMAN: Amos was talkin' to Eben Smith. He's just back from a trip to El-a-noy. Come to get his folks.

2ND WOMAN: El-a-noy? Where's that?

1ST WOMAN: Over past Indiana. Not a bad trip, Amos says. And the soil! He never saw such soil! He's tellin' everyone. Reckon half the county will be movin' out. We're goin', Amos and I. (*As the* WOMEN *exit, a group of* PIONEERS *come in singing "El-a-noy."**)

PIONEERS:

"Way down upon the Wabash,
Such land was never known" . . . (*Etc.*) (*As* PIONEERS *finish song, they should go into a lively square dance. Or, if this does not seem practicable, one of the* PIONEERS *might strum "Oh, Susanna!" on a guitar. As the* PIO-

NEERS *exit,* CHORUS *again repeats "I am bound for the promised land.")*

NARRATOR: Sing of pioneers discovering gold in California in 1849, and in the Rocky Mountains ten years later. Sing of picks and shovels and tin pans scraping the creek bottoms . . . and wild eyes and fevered brows. Sing of fortunes made and fortunes lost, and America amazing the world with the abundance of her resources. Sing of more and more stars added to the flag as the west was opened up.

CHORUS: West Virginia . . . Nevada . . . Nebraska . . . Colorado.

NARRATOR: The country was filling up, the homesteads were being taken. Where millions of buffalo had roamed a few years before, cows grazed in green pastures. Where buffalo grass had curled rich and sweet over the prairies, corn and wheat were growing. Our country was a flower unfolding—an American Beauty rose. (CHORUS *sings stanza of "America the Beautiful."*) Sing, America, of whistles . . . (*Sound of various whistles offstage, if possible.*) Factory whistles, mine whistles, mill whistles, train whistles. And sing of wheels—spinning wheels, wagon wheels, paddlewheels, wheels of engines and locomotives. And sing, America, of hoofs . . . the hoofs of cows and oxen, and horses and mules. Sing of the mustang horses driven up the Chisholm Trail and the millions of longhorn cattle. (COWBOYS *come in twirling ropes, singing "The Chisholm Trail."**)

SOLO COWBOY:

"Well, come along boys and listen to my tale,

I'll tell you of my troubles on the Old Chisholm Trail."

COWBOYS: "Coma ti yi youpy . . ." (*Etc.*)

2ND SOLO COWBOY:

"Oh! it's bacon and beans 'most every day,

I'd as soon be a-eatin' prairie hay."

COWBOYS: "Coma ti yi youpy . . ." (*Etc.*)

3RD SOLO COWBOY:

"I went up to the boss to draw my roll,
He had it figgered out I was nine dollars in the hole."

COWBOYS: "Coma ti yi youpy . . ." (*Etc.*)

4TH SOLO:

"My seat is in the saddle and my saddle's in the sky,
An' I'll quit punchin' cows in the sweet bye and bye."

COWBOYS: "Coma ti yi youpy . . ." (*Etc.*) (*As they go
out twirling their ropes,* CHORUS *sings "Goodbye, Old
Paint."**)

CHORUS:

"Goodbye, old Paint, I'm a-leavin' Cheyenne . . ."
(*Etc.*)

NARRATOR: In just two years, 1889 and 1890, six new states
came into the Union:

CHORUS: North Dakota . . . South Dakota . . . Montana
. . . Washington . . . Idaho . . . Wyoming.

NARRATOR: And sing of three more states added to the
Union by 1912—Oklahoma, New Mexico, and Arizona.
Our flag that started so gallantly with thirteen stars
showed forty-eight. Forty-eight stars on a field of blue,
next to thirteen stripes of red and white.

CHORUS (*Speaking*):

Red for courage to do the right,
White for faith with its guiding light,
Blue for strength in carrying-through
Hail—to the red and white and blue!

NARRATOR: And then came another war, the First World
War . . . and we were there, hoping to make the world
safe for democracy—the kind of democracy we had and
cherished. Our men were on the march again, in a
strange land this time, with unfamiliar names.

CHORUS (*Staccato*): The Somme . . . Verdun . . . Capo-
retto . . . the Aisne . . . the Meuse-Argonne.

NARRATOR: Our men were on the march. (SOLDIERS *come in marching, single file, a continuous line across stage, as* CHORUS *sings, "Over There"*)

CHORUS (*At end of song, staccato*): Knit . . . make bandages . . . mail packages . . . write letters . . . keep the home fires burning . . . and pray!

NARRATOR: Sing, America, of November 11, 1918, the Armistice signed, and our boys on their way back home. (CHORUS *puts on an Armistice Day demonstration, waving flags, shouting, tooting horns, making a great deal of noise.* SOLDIERS *come marching back singing "Hinky Dinky."**) Sing, America, of peace again, and our country moving ahead. Automobiles on the highways. Radios in the living rooms. And chicken every Sunday. Sing of the age of the common man, the working man coming into his own. And then another war, World War II, so close on the heels of the last! (SOLDIERS *cross stage again, this time singing "Praise the Lord and Pass the Ammunition."*)

CHORUS: Pearl Harbor . . . Bataan . . . Corregidor . . . Guadalcanal . . . the Aleutians . . . the Battle of the Bulge . . . the atom bomb! (STAGEHAND *enters with sign:* ANY TOWN, U.S.A., AUG. 6, 1945. *He exits as* RADIO VOICE *comes over loudspeaker.*)

RADIO VOICE: This morning the first atom bomb in history was dropped on Hiroshima, Japan! It will be impossible to tell the extent of the destruction for days . . . possibly months. Scientists estimate that at least half the population of the city and more than half the buildings have been destroyed. Dropped from an American plane, the bomb came as a complete surprise. What the effect of this new weapon of warfare will be, no one can say at this moment. (RADIO VOICE *off, as* TWO WOMEN *enter.*)

1ST WOMAN: I don't like it.

2ND WOMAN: It was the quickest way to end the war, Elizabeth. Japan can't hold out now.

1ST WOMAN: But I don't believe man should have such power in his hands.

2ND WOMAN: Well, he has it.

1ST WOMAN: There's only a one-way street ahead for us now. We've got to use the atom for *peace,* not war. For building up, not tearing down. It's the world's only salvation.

2ND WOMAN: Atoms for peace—that's not a bad idea. But . . .

1ST WOMAN: There can't be any "but." It's civilization's only hope. That, and the U.N. Let me tell you, the days of the pioneer aren't over. We have new frontiers to conquer—glorious frontiers.

2ND WOMAN: What do you mean, Elizabeth?

1ST WOMAN: The frontiers of a new age . . . the atomic age that lies ahead, just around the corner. We can make this world a better world than it has ever been before. (*The* TWO WOMEN *go out;* STAGEHAND *enters and removes sign. Exits.*)

NARRATOR: Sing, America, sing of the fifty stars on our new flag; and of the strength of our Union. Sing of atoms for peace. Sing of our United States as part of the United Nations, helping to make the world a place of peace and safety, a place of plenty and opportunity for everyone. Sing of what free men can do for the cause of freedom. (CHORUS *sings "A New Wind A-Blowin'."* *)

CHORUS:
"There's a brand new wind a-blowin' down the Lincoln road.

There's a brand new hope a-growin' where freedom's seeds are sowed . . ." (*Etc.*)

NARRATOR: Sing, America. Sing of the freedom that is ours to cherish. Sing of songs unwritten and of great words said. Sing of the spirit that must never perish. Sing of the road well-traveled, and the road ahead. Sing, America, sing! (SAILORS, PIONEERS, COWBOYS, SOLDIERS, *etc., come back on stage as everyone sings "God Bless America."*)

THE END

Sing the Songs of Freedom

Characters

(Many parts may be doubled up)

MASTER OF CEREMONIES	AARON
FIRST BOY	HARTLEY
FIRST GIRL	JOSEPH HOPKINSON
SECOND GIRL	EMILY HOPKINSON
SECOND BOY	GILBERT FOX
CHORUS	DR. BEANES
MARY WILLIAMS	FRANCIS SCOTT KEY
RACHEL	SAMUEL FRANCIS SMITH
SARAH	CONFEDERATE BOYS
CHARLES NORRIS	UNION BOYS
JOHN DICKINSON	NEGRO WOMEN
SONS OF LIBERTY	WORKMEN
LOUDSPEAKER VOICE	EMMA LAZARUS
JED	LEAH

TIME: *The present.*

SETTING: *Auditorium stage with stand for* M.C., *chairs for* CHORUS *at back.*

AT RISE: M.C. *and* CHORUS *are in places on stage.*

M.C.: Friends, our program for today revolves around a small two-syllable word that is one of the biggest and

---

All songs in this play (except "America") can be found in *The Fireside Book of Favorite American Songs* by Boni, Lloyd and Battaglia (Simon and Schuster, 1952).

most important words in the world. Wars have been fought over it. Billions of dollars have been spent for it and against it. Millions upon millions of people have been, and now are, involved in striving for it and trying to preserve it. The word is *freedom*.

Does it seem strange to you that we teen-agers have chosen the theme of freedom for our program—we who have been accused so often of taking the blessings of liberty for granted? We who are supposed to be so pre-occupied with having a good time that we forget about serious things!

It is true that freedom has come to our generation the easy way. We are privileged to live in a democracy that has been handed down to us as a gift tied with a golden ribbon. We have not had to lift a finger to win this freedom. Some of our ancestors, even some of our fathers, fought for it, and died for it. But we face the space age with this gift in our hands. Do we appreciate it? Do we value it enough? Do we intend to preserve it?

We hope, by the end of this program, that you will know our answer without reservation. We hope you will see that although we are accused of being careless and selfish, we do not think that life is just an amusement park.

In case you are wondering, here is how we got the idea for the program in the first place. Several weeks ago one of our boys happened upon some lines he had never read before. (FIRST BOY *enters, with open book.*)

FIRST BOY: "Years of the modern! Years of the unper-form'd! Your horizon rises, I see it parting away for more august dramas,

"I see not America only, not only Liberty's nation but other nations preparing,

"I see tremendous entrances and exits, new combinations, the solidarity of races . . . (FIRST GIRL *enters from other side of stage, stands listening.*)

"I see Freedom . . . with Law on one side and Peace on the other . . ."

FIRST GIRL: What are you reading?

FIRST BOY: It's called "Years of the Modern."

FIRST GIRL: "Years of the Modern!" That means your years and mine. (*Gestures to include audience*) Our years. "Tremendous entrances and exits" fits in with where we stand, facing the space age, doesn't it? Who's the new poet?

FIRST BOY (*Evasively, reading*): "Never were such sharp questions ask'd as this day . . ." (SECOND GIRL *comes in, stands near* FIRST GIRL.)

FIRST GIRL: He talks a language we can understand. What does he think lies ahead for us?

FIRST BOY (*Reading*): "No one knows what will happen next, such portents fill the days and nights."

SECOND GIRL: What in the world are you two talking about?

FIRST GIRL: About a new poet, looking into our future.

SECOND BOY (*Coming in, standing near* FIRST BOY): What new poet? (*Looks over* FIRST BOY's *shoulder, laughs*) New? We studied him in English last year. Don't you remember? (*Recites dramatically*)

"Sail, sail thy best, ship of Democracy!
Of value is thy freight—'tis not the Present only,
The Past is also stored in thee!"

FIRST GIRL: That's Walt Whitman, isn't it?

FIRST BOY: A gold star for your diploma.

SECOND GIRL: What do you mean, he's looking into *our* future? Walt Whitman wrote a hundred years ago.

FIRST BOY: But the past is also stored in the present, remember. And in the future, too. Someone has figured out that in the course of world history twenty or more different civilizations have risen—risen and fallen. All have fallen but ours. The problem we're facing now is how to make ours last. History should help us out.

FIRST GIRL: Ours is a good civilization. We *have* to make it last. And if going back into the past will help, let's go!

SECOND BOY: How far?

FIRST BOY: Far enough to become reacquainted with America's most vital weapon.

SECOND GIRL: Most vital weapon? Rockets? Guided missiles? But they're new. What do you mean—reacquainted?

FIRST BOY (*Slowly*): The most vital weapon we have, or ever will have, hasn't anything to do with rockets. It's our *heritage of freedom.* "Life, Liberty and the pursuit of Happiness!"

FIRST GIRL: That's true—when you come to think of it. I guess we just don't think about freedom enough, though.

FIRST BOY: To preserve our freedom we have to preserve our democracy—as the only way to meet the "tremendous entrances and exits" ahead.

SECOND BOY *and* SECOND GIRL: But what can we do?

FIRST GIRL: We can't sit back and take our blessings for granted, that's certain.

FIRST BOY: No, we can't. We have to treasure the ideals of justice, liberty, and respect for the individual. We must keep our freedom of speech, freedom of worship, and freedom from tyranny, and make these things count in our lives and other people's lives.

SECOND BOY: All right. I'm for broadcasting the songs of freedom all over town!

FIRST BOY: Not only the songs, but the spirit that prompted them in the first place.

FIRST GIRL: Say, we've been trying to think of something appropriate for our graduation program.* Why not use the songs of freedom as our theme?

SECOND GIRL: Let's!

SECOND BOY: Come on, what are we waiting for? (*They hurry out.*)

M.C.: And so, friends, today we are singing the songs of freedom. Today we are going back into the past to recapture the spirit of men and women who made our country the land of the free.

CHORUS:
"My country, 'tis of thee,
Sweet land of liberty,
Of thee I sing;
Land where my fathers died,
Land of the Pilgrims' pride,
From every mountain side
Let Freedom ring."

M.C.: Let Freedom ring as it did along the Atlantic seaboard in the early days of our settlement! Let it ring —though men be banished to the wilderness for speaking out on the side of liberty and the rights of man! (*Pauses, changes tone*) The time is 1636, late January, of a cold and snowy year. The place is Salem, Massachusetts. (MARY WILLIAMS, RACHEL *and* SARAH *enter.*) The wife of Roger Williams is talking with two friends who have come to call.

MARY: My husband always said it was unbelievable how God's children could persecute God's children.

SARAH: It's ridiculous that the Puritans, who came to these shores to find religious freedom, should deny that same freedom to others. Your husband is a courageous man, Mary. Everyone knows that Roger Williams will speak his mind no matter what the consequences.

---

* May be changed to fit the occasion—class day, etc.

RACHEL (*Gloomily*): I dread to think of the consequences in this case.

SARAH: Most of us are courageous only to a point—a point we consider safe for our comfort and security. But not Brother Williams. He will do anything to promote the cause of freedom. Imagine his standing up and telling the Council that Church and State must be separated— when the Council now rules both Church and State! Imagine his contending that everyone should be allowed to worship according to his own conscience, when the Puritans are bent on forcing their own beliefs on everyone. Why, Brother Williams even dares to talk to the Council about democracy!

RACHEL: How long has it been, Mary, since he had to flee in that dreadful snowstorm?

MARY: Eight days. And still no word from him!

SARAH: The baseness of the Council! After giving him until spring to leave the colony, then to decide suddenly to seize him and ship him off to England! And he so ill with the fever.

MARY (*Desperately*): Do you think—is it possible—that a sick man could drag himself through such a blizzard— sixty miles to the nearest camp of friendly Indians?

SARAH: Of course, it's possible. No one knows the wilderness like your husband, Mary. If anyone could escape to safety, he is the one. He wasn't doubtful, was he?

MARY: No. But his faith is greater than mine.

SARAH: How fearful the Council must be that he will plant some seeds of democracy amongst us!

RACHEL (*Gloomily*): Having to flee and leave all his worldly goods behind—to say nothing of his wife and two small daughters.

MARY: We are to join him when he starts the new colony in the spring.

RACHEL: A sick man making his way through a blizzard.

SARAH: You can be sure he was grateful for the storm. It would blot out his footprints. It would confuse his pursuers. Why, I can just see Brother Williams forcing his way ahead, singing in the storm.

MARY (*Nodding*): His favorite hymn—"We Gather Together." He was especially fond of the last stanza.

SARAH: Let's sing it for him now!

MARY, RACHEL, SARAH (*Singing last stanza of "We Gather Together"*):
"We all do extol Thee, Thou Leader in battle,
And pray that Thou still our Defender wilt be.
Let Thy congregation escape tribulation;
Thy name be ever praised! O Lord, make us free!" (*Exit, repeating the last line.*)

M.C.: Roger Williams, fevered and hungry, made his way through the blizzard to the camp of friendly Narragansetts. The following spring, on land purchased from the Indians, he started a colony at Providence, Rhode Island, promising religious freedom to all. The constitution he helped draw up for the colony was the first democratic one in America.

CHORUS:
"Thy name be ever praised! O Lord, make us free!"

M.C.: The next milestone in our freedom came in 1735. John Peter Zenger, after enduring months of imprisonment in a dark clammy cell, was declared not guilty of libeling the royal governor in his newspaper. The case was really a test of strength between a tyrannical colonial governor and the people. For the first time, a printer's right to publish the unvarnished truth about the government was upheld by a court. A milestone for freedom of speech!

CHORUS:
"Thy name be ever praised! O Lord, make us free!"

M.C.: Freedom is a jewel with many facets: Freedom to

worship as one pleases, freedom to speak the truth, and then—freedom from tyranny. (*Pauses, changes tone*) It is the spring of 1768. John Dickinson, a Pennsylvania lawyer, is talking to his friend, Charles Norris of Philadelphia. (NORRIS *and* DICKINSON *enter.*) Both men are disturbed by the continuing crisis between England and the American colonies. Trouble had started three years before when England passed the Stamp Act, imposing a system of tax duties on the colonists.

NORRIS: You're too mild in your opposition, Mr. Dickinson.

DICKINSON: I don't believe in violent resistance. I'm doing my best to point out the evils of British policy in a quiet way.

NORRIS: Too quiet, too quiet. What we need is something rousing like a good patriotic song!

DICKINSON: We may have to resort to force in the end, but I still think we can work out this thing peaceably.

NORRIS: How?

DICKINSON: By refusing to import British goods, for one thing. And by refusing to export our goods to Britain. Loss of trade is something English merchants can understand. Rattling our swords will only make them laugh. After all, Mr. Norris, we're fewer than three million here in America—with all too many on the side of England.

NORRIS: I still think we need something more telling than economic pressure. With your ability as a writer, John Dickinson, you could do something to spark the patriots. Can't you think of a stirring song to pass along to James Otis for the Sons of Liberty? You used to write poems, I remember.

DICKINSON: I have long since renounced poetry. Still— (*Shrugs as they go out.*)

M.C.: A few days later John Dickinson wrote to James Otis, patriot leader in Massachusetts: "I enclose you a song for American freedom." It was "The Liberty Song," our first patriotic American song. Very quickly it became the rallying cry for patriots up and down the Atlantic seaboard. (*Several* SONS OF LIBERTY *come in singing "The Liberty Song."*)

SONS OF LIBERTY:

"Come join hand in hand, brave Americans all,
And rouse your bold hearts at fair Liberty's call;
No tyrannous acts shall suppress your just claim,
Or stain with dishonor America's name."

CHORUS (*Joining in*):

"In Freedom we're born and in Freedom we'll live.
Our purses are ready.
Steady, friends, steady;
Not as slaves, but as free men our money we'll give."

SONS OF LIBERTY:

"Then join hand in hand, brave Americans all,
By uniting we stand, by dividing we fall;
In so righteous a cause let us hope to succeed,
For heaven approves of each generous deed."

CHORUS (*Joining in*): "In Freedom we're born," *etc.*

M.C.: The following year, 1769, John Adams made this entry in his diary:

LOUDSPEAKER VOICE: "Dined with 350 Sons of Liberty in Robinson's Tavern in Dorchester. There was a large collection of good company. We had *The Liberty Song* (Dickinson's) and the whole company joined in the chorus." (CHORUS *and* SONS OF LIBERTY *repeat chorus.* SONS OF LIBERTY *exit.*)

M.C.: In the spring of 1775 the Revolutionary War began. A month before the first shots were fired at Lexington and Concord, Patrick Henry made history in the revo-

lutionary convention of Virginia. He burst into an elo-
quent speech with a ring of defiance that echoes down
the years.

LOUDSPEAKER VOICE: "Shall we gather strength by irresolu-
tion and inaction? Shall we acquire the means of effec-
tual resistance by lying supinely on our backs, and hug-
ging the delusive phantom of hope, until our enemies
shall have bound us hand and foot? . . . The battle is
not to the strong alone, it is to the vigilant, the active,
the brave. . . . Is life so dear, or peace so sweet, as to be
purchased at the price of chains and slavery?"

M.C.: Soon General Washington took command of the
colonial army, and raw recruits began to train. Men sang
"The Liberty Song" and marched to the lively strains
of "Yankee Doodle"—a tune they had taken over from
the British. Freedom was the star on the horizon and our
poor little army struggled toward it. (*Pauses*) Late in the
year 1777, a small, discouraged American army is forced
to retire to Valley Forge, Pennsylvania. Things have not
been going well for General Washington. He has been
defeated at Brandywine. He has lost Philadelphia, and
the British are moving in for the winter. He has just
barely escaped from the enemy at Germantown. As
night falls, the troops make camp a few miles east of
Valley Forge. Three young soldiers, tired, ragged, hungry, gather wood for their fire.

JED (*Coming in with something between two sticks*):
Where's the wood? Hurry! I have a smouldering stick.

AARON (*Coming with wood*): Here. It's not very dry.
(*Fixes sticks*) I'll hold my coat around and you blow.

HARTLEY (*Hurrying in*): Wait, I've found some dry leaves
and pine needles. (*Sets leaves between sticks. They
stoop around fire.*)

JED (*Holding out hands*): Lord, that's good.

AARON (*Disgruntled*): What's good? That the British got our nice warm quarters in Philadelphia?

HARTLEY: Maybe they got our quarters, Aaron, but they didn't get us. (CHORUS *starts humming tune of "Chester."*)

JED: There's that song again, "Chester." The song of the Revolution! It's almost as good as a fire.

AARON: Good for what? For starving to the tune of it?

JED: For reminding us what we're fighting for, that's what. Freedom from tyranny! Freedom to live our own lives in our own way! By the way, Hartley, I found out who wrote that song. You were wondering. Fellow named William Billings. A tanner, born in Boston.

HARTLEY: A tanner?

JED: Yes. With very little education. Just a natural born musicmaker, and a patriot.

AARON: What company is he in?

JED: He's not in the army.

AARON: Thought you said he was a patriot?

JED: Look, Aaron. He's deformed. One leg shorter than the other, and one arm withered. And blind in one eye. He's worse off than we are, but he keeps making music for us to sing.

HARTLEY: Listen—listen to them sing. Tired, hungry, nothing but rags on our backs—and we're singing!

JED *and* HARTLEY (*Stand and sing to the tune of "Chester"*):

"Let tyrants shake their iron rod,
And Slav'ry clank her galling chains.
We fear them not; we trust in God,
New England's God forever reigns."

AARON (*Moved, stands and joins in*):

"The Foe comes on with haughty stride.
Our troops advance with martial noise.

Their Vet'rans flee before our Youth,
And Gen'rals yield to beardless boys."

(CHORUS *joins in, repeating last two lines above.*)

HARTLEY: That sounds like men who have something to fight for. Freedom! What if we *are* tired and hungry? That's only for a day, a week. Freedom's for a good long time.

JED (*Pointing off-stage*): There's the mess sergeant with some bread, you beardless boys. Bread! (*They hurry out.*)

M.C.: The war for independence was fought and won. After considerable debate and bickering, the Constitution of the United States of America was signed—to secure the blessings of liberty.

Our new country began to stretch and develop economically and politically. Eli Whitney invented the cotton gin. Charles Newbold took out a patent for an iron plow. Political parties came into being—the party of Jefferson as opposed to followers of Hamilton and John Adams. And in the meantime friction developed with England and France over trade, boundaries, and frontier incidents. (*Pause*) One spring evening in 1798, in Philadelphia, Joseph Hopkinson, a young lawyer, is reading the evening paper. (JOSEPH *enters, shaking head over paper. He puts it down when his wife comes in.* EMILY *enters.*)

JOSEPH: Oh, why must we have all this hostility in our new country! Instead of everyone working together for America's greatness, one group is bitterly anti-French, another as bitterly anti-British. It seems to me that war with France is inevitable if this goes on.

EMILY: Don't worry so, Joseph. (*Soothingly*) How did things go at the office today?

JOSEPH (*Calming down*): Wait till I tell you, Emily.

(*Laughs*) You'll be amused. In my seven years of practice I never had such a request as came to me today.

EMILY: A new case?

JOSEPH: Hardly a case. Remember that young Englishman we met at the Fine Arts Ball last year? Gilbert Fox. (EMILY *nods*.) I've talked to him on several occasions. A likable chap. He has recently joined the company of the Chestnut Street Theater as a singer. It's in that capacity that he came to see me today.

EMILY: Does a singer need a lawyer?

JOSEPH: No, but he needs a song.

EMILY: I don't understand.

JOSEPH (*Laughing*): My dear Emily, he wants me to write him a song for a benefit performance. To the tune of "The President's March." Did you ever hear of anything more ridiculous?

EMILY (*Seriously*): You could do it, you know.

JOSEPH: I? What could I write a song about?

EMILY: Something that stirs you deeply, something that would impel you to write spirited words.

JOSEPH: Why, that's exactly what Fox said! But what could stir me enough to make me a poet?

EMILY: Not a day passes but you speak of the need for unity in our new United States, Joseph. If you could put some of your ideas across in a song, think how much good it might do.

JOSEPH (*Excited*): I'll try! By Jove, I'll try. To arouse an American spirit would be something worth doing. (*He hurries out.* EMILY *follows.*)

M.C.: And so Joseph Hopkinson wrote his song and Gilbert Fox sang it in the Chestnut Street Theater a few nights later.

FOX (*Coming in, singing "Hail, Columbia"*):
"Hail, Columbia, happy land,

Hail, ye heroes, heav'n-born band,
Who fought and bled in Freedom's cause,
Who fought and bled in Freedom's cause,
And when the storm of war was gone,
Enjoy'd the peace your valor won.
Let independence be our boast,
Ever mindful what it cost,
Ever grateful for the prize,
Let its altar reach the skies."

CHORUS (*Joining in*):
"Firm, united let us be,
Rallying round our liberty,
As a band of brothers join'd,
Peace and safety we shall find."
(*If desired,* Fox *may sing another stanza of "Hail, Columbia," with* CHORUS *again joining in on chorus.* Fox *exits.*)

M.C.: Joseph Hopkinson's song, "Hail, Columbia," was received with great enthusiasm, and his object of getting Americans to rise above their passions and prejudices was to a great extent attained. Now, more than a century and a half later, Joseph Hopkinson's claim to fame rests more upon his "Hail, Columbia" than upon his notable success as a lawyer and judge. (*Pause*)

We move along sixteen years, to something that happened during the War of 1812, when we were fighting to maintain our freedom. We could not permit the British to prey on our commerce, seize our sailors, and stir up the Indians to attack our frontier. And so in June, 1812, Congress declared war on England. More than two years later we were still fighting.

CHORUS:
"Firm, united let us be,
Rallying round our liberty . . ." (*Etc.*)

M.C.: It is before dawn on the morning of September 14,

1814. Francis Scott Key, a young Washington attorney, is anxiously watching from the deck of a small American boat anchored in Chesapeake Bay. (KEY *enters*) There are British battleships on either side. The afternoon before, Mr. Key and a government agent had made arrangements for the release of an American prisoner who had been seized by the British on their retreat from Washington. But the British, about to attack Fort McHenry which guarded the city of Baltimore, refused to let the Americans return to shore until after the bombardment. The firing has been going on throughout the night. While Mr. Key strains to see the fort, the released prisoner, Dr. Beanes, a prominent physician, enters. (BEANES *enters*.)

BEANES: Still watching and waiting, Mr. Key?

KEY: That you, Doctor? Yes, still hoping for another glimpse of the stars and stripes on the fort. Did you get some sleep?

BEANES: A little. I suppose the relief of being free again, after more than a fortnight of anxiety as a British prisoner, enabled me to sleep in spite of the noise. They've kept up the firing, haven't they?

KEY: All night. And what if the fort falls, Doctor? Last month the British burned a good deal of Washington. This month is it to be Baltimore? And next month? What will happen to our country if its leading cities fall to the enemy?

BEANES: The flag was still there during the night. We saw it several times by the light of the rockets.

KEY: But this morning! The suspense is agony. We have made ourselves a nation here in America, a free nation. Have we the ability to preserve it? I feel our cause is just, and I believe in the power of justice to prevail. Still, I'd feel better if I saw the stars and stripes still waving.

BEANES: Dawn will be breaking soon.

KEY: I don't know when I've been so anxious as this night. There's so much at stake, Doctor—our flag, our country, our freedom. (*Suddenly points*) Look! There through the mist! Isn't that the flag?

BEANES: I believe it is.

KEY: Then Fort McHenry still stands. Baltimore is safe. The flag still waves! (*They exit.*)

M.C.: On his way back to shore that morning, Francis Scott Key wrote down on the back of an envelope the words and phrases that had filled his mind during the long anxious night. The words took the form of a poem which began, "O say, can you see, by the dawn's early light, What so proudly we hailed at the twilight's last gleaming . . ." The next day Mr. Key showed the poem to his friend Judge Nicholson in Baltimore. The Judge and his wife were so enthusiastic they had copies printed and circulated. Soon "The Star-Spangled Banner" was being sung throughout the young nation. Its popularity has never waned. In 1931, Congress officially made it our national anthem.

CHORUS (*Singing last stanza*):
  "O! thus be it ever, when freemen shall stand . . ." (*Etc.*)

M.C.: Freedom marches on. In 1832, a song written within half an hour became one of the most popular patriotic songs ever written in the United States. In fact, it has for years been popularly called our national hymn. Its author, a 24-year-old divinity student, met some of his school expenses by translating and writing. He had graduated from Harvard three years before in the class of Oliver Wendell Holmes, and of him Holmes had quipped:

LOUDSPEAKER VOICE: "And there's a nice youngster of excellent pith:
  Fate tried to conceal him by naming him Smith."

M.C.: But young Samuel Francis Smith was not to be concealed. In 1832, he received a letter from the president of the Handel and Haydn Society in Boston asking him to translate or compose verses for a song book. (SMITH *enters, looking through pages of letter.*)

SMITH: For a song book to be used in the schools. Hmmm. Here's a nice tune. German words. (*Hums snatches of tune of "America."*) Patriotic. (*Looks up*) Why couldn't I use the tune for a patriotic song about America? About the land of freedom? I'll get some paper. (*Exits*)

M.C.: Smith wrote his song, and before the year was out it appeared in the new song book. The tune was an old one, well-known in England and Germany. But Smith's words were new for a new country. The success of "America" was immediate.

CHORUS (*Singing second stanza of "America"*):
"My native country, thee,
Land of the noble free . . ." (*Etc.*)

M.C.: Land of the noble free! But not always so free, and not always so noble. There was no freedom for the Negroes who had been seized in Africa and transported like animals to our Atlantic seaboard. As early as 1770, when we were chafing under British tyranny, one-sixth of our country's population were Negro slaves, chafing under the mastery of individual owners in the South, where slavery was part of the plantation system. Everyone knows how the slavery question became a more and more burning issue in every political campaign from the Missouri Compromise of 1820 until the Civil War. The question finally had to be settled on the battlefield, our country split asunder, North fighting against South. Never had union been so threatened, never was democracy in such danger. Abraham Lincoln spoke out forcefully.

LOUDSPEAKER VOICE: "As I would not be a *slave*, so I

would not be a *master*. This expresses my idea of democracy. Whatever differs from this, to the extent of the difference, is no democracy.

"I would save the Union. I would save it in the shortest way under the Constitution. . . . My paramount object in this struggle is to save the Union.

"Plainly the sheep and the wolf are not agreed upon a definition of liberty."

M.C.: The South had its own national anthem, extolling the rights of a band of brothers fighting for their liberty. (*Several* CONFEDERATE BOYS *carrying the Confederate flag come in singing "The Bonnie Blue Flag."*)

CONFEDERATE BOYS:

"We are a band of brothers, and native to the soil,
Fighting for our liberty with treasure, blood, and toil;
And when our rights were threat'ned, the cry rose near and far:
Hurrah! for the Bonnie Blue Flag, that bears a Single Star." (*They stand at one side of stage.*)

M.C.: The North also had its songs. George Root's "The Battle Cry of Freedom," written a few hours after President Lincoln's call for troops, immediately became popular throughout the North, with its stirring words.

CHORUS (*Chanting*):

"Yes, we'll rally round the flag, boys, we'll rally once again,
Shouting the battle cry of Freedom,
We'll rally from the hillside, we'll gather from the plain,
Shouting the battle cry of Freedom!"

M.C.: Another of George Root's songs became a famous marching song for the Boys in Blue. (UNION BOYS *come marching in carrying the Stars and Stripes, singing.*)

UNION BOYS:

"Tramp, tramp, tramp, the boys are marching,
Cheer up, comrades, they will come (they will come)

And beneath the starry flag we shall breathe the air again
Of the free land in our own beloved home." (UNION
Boys *stand opposite* CONFEDERATE Boys.)

M.C.: And sometimes both North and South, weary of
fighting, hoping for peace and unity again, would sing
the same songs, like the nostalgic "Just Before the Battle,
Mother."

CONFEDERATE BOYS *and* UNION BOYS:
"Hark! I hear the bugle calling,
'Tis the signal for the fight;
Now may God protect us, Mother,
As He ever does the right.
Hear the 'Battle Cry of Freedom,'
How it swells upon the air!
Oh yes, we'll rally 'round the standard,
Or we'll perish nobly there." (*They exit together, re-
peating the last few lines as they march out.*)

M.C.: And then the war between the states was over. The
Union had been saved. Lincoln's "government of the
people, by the people, for the people" was going to have
another chance. (*Several* NEGRO WOMEN *cross stage singing jubilantly, "Oh, Freedom."*)

NEGRO WOMEN:
"Oh, freedom! Oh, freedom!
Oh, freedom over me!
And before I'll be a slave,
I'll be buried in my grave,
An' go home to my Lord an' be free." (*They exit.*)

M.C.: Following the Civil War, a new era began, an
era of expansion and industrial development. The West
was being opened up. Those who stayed respectably at
home in the East sang sentimental parlor songs like
"Silver Threads Among the Gold" and "The Old
Oaken Bucket." But the pioneers, the lumberjacks, the
steel drivers, the cowboys, who helped push our frontiers

westward, sang new songs of freedom to work and freedom to move around.

The campaign for shorter working hours began soon
after the end of the War between the States, but it was
not until the '80's that the campaign for an 8-hour day
gained momentum. At labor's first May Day celebration in 1886, a song called "Eight Hours" was adopted
as the official song of the movement. (WORKMEN *enter
singing "Eight Hours."*)

WORKMEN:

"We mean to make things over, we are tired of toil for
    naught,
With but bare enough to live upon and ne'er an hour for
    thought;
We want to feel the sunshine, and we want to smell the
    flow'rs,
We are sure that God has willed it, and we mean to have
    eight hours.
We're summoning our forces from the shipyard, shop,
    and mill."

CHORUS (*Joining in*):

"Eight hours for work, eight hours for rest,
Eight hours for what we will,
Eight hours for work, eight hours for rest,
Eight hours for what we will." (WORKMEN *exit on last
    two lines.*)

M.C.: The freedom America stood for was talked about
around the world. Freedom of speech and religion. Freedom of work and movement. Freedom to live without
fear of tyranny. Freedom to get ahead, to become somebody. All these existed in large measure in our country,
so rich in natural resources. Immigrants poured in, in
increasing numbers. Listen to the figures.

LOUDSPEAKER VOICE: Between 1821 and 1830—107,000 immigrants. Between 1851 and 1860—2,453,000. Between

1881 and 1890—4,737,000. Between 1901 and 1910—8,136,000.

M.C.: In 1886 the people of France presented us with a symbol of what our country stood for. They gave us a colossal statue, to stand on an island in New York harbor where all incoming and outgoing ships could see it. The Statue of Liberty! (*Pause*) Let's look in at the home of a wealthy New York family in the summer of the year the statue was presented. A young woman of 36, a successful writer and friend of Emerson, is much affected by the implications of this gift from France. Her name is Emma Lazarus. She is talking earnestly to a friend. (EMMA *and* LEAH *enter*.)

EMMA: Think how the oppressed peoples of Europe will feel when they see the statue, Leah! The Statue of Liberty, with its torch of freedom held high.

LEAH: It's strange how deeply you feel about these things, Emma. You've always had wealth, a devoted family, happiness. Yet you put yourself in the place of refugees and poor immigrants and know how they must feel.

EMMA: Is that so strange?

LEAH: You organize campaigns for refugee relief, and you write articles defending oppressed peoples. You do more than anyone I know.

EMMA: It's little enough. (*Takes paper from pocket*) I've written a few words about the new statue, Leah. A sonnet. What do you think of it? (*Hands paper to* LEAH)

LEAH (*After reading silently for a few minutes, aloud*): "Give me your tired, your poor,
Your huddled masses yearning to breathe free,
The wretched refuse of your teeming shore,
Send these, the homeless, tempest-tossed, to me:
I lift my lamp beside the golden door." (LEAH *looks up, much affected.*) It's wonderful. (*Arm in arm,* EMMA *and* LEAH *cross stage slowly and exit.*)

M.C.: The poem to the Statue of Liberty by Emma Lazarus was chosen to be engraved on a tablet for the pedestal of the statue before the year was out. It can still be read there by visitors to Liberty Island.

CHORUS:

"Let music swell the breeze,
And ring from all the trees
Sweet Freedom's song . . ."

M.C.: And then came the twentieth century—and two world wars. Dictators challenged democracy, tried to sweep it from the face of the earth, tried to force upon defenseless countries a rule of might instead of a rule of right. America could not sit and watch with folded hands. In his message to Congress in April, 1917, President Wilson declared:

LOUDSPEAKER VOICE: "The world must be made safe for democracy. Its peace must be planted upon the tested foundations of political liberty."

M.C.: And later the same year, when we were fighting by the side of our freedom-loving allies, President Wilson said:

LOUDSPEAKER VOICE: "We have been given the opportunity to serve mankind as we once served ourselves in the great days of our Declaration of Independence. . . . In this day of the revelation of our duty not only to defend our own rights as a nation but to defend also the rights of free men throughout the world . . . a new light shines about us. The great duties of a new day awaken a new and greater national spirit in us."

M.C.: We met the same challenge in the Second World War. And now, my friends, at the advent of the space age, the challenge is with us again. Our differences with dictators have not been resolved. Communism promises the hungry nations of the world freedom from poverty, but would deny them the other freedoms we enjoy. Will we have the foresight and courage to help struggling countries gain the four freedoms made famous by President Roosevelt—freedom of speech, freedom of worship, freedom from want, freedom from fear? (FIRST BOY, FIRST GIRL, SECOND BOY, *and* SECOND GIRL *have appeared at one side of stage during this speech. Now they come forward.*)

FIRST BOY: This is where we come in.

M.C.: You?

FIRST BOY: This is where the present joins the past, and learns from it. This is where the future begins.

FIRST GIRL: We represent the "Years of the Modern," ready to take part in the tremendous entrances and exits ahead.

SECOND GIRL: We want to see to it that the years ahead will be good years.

SECOND BOY: We want to keep Freedom with Law on one side and Peace on the other, as Walt Whitman prophesied.

M.C. (*Stepping away from stand*): The stage is yours. May the blessings of history be upon you! (*Gestures to* CHORUS) All we have here is the past, with its precious legacy of ideals realized. Have you a cue to the future, my friends?

FIRST BOY: Yes. A cue and a watchword.

FIRST *and* SECOND GIRLS: "I see not America only, not only Liberty's nation but other nations preparing."

FIRST *and* SECOND BOYS: "I see tremendous entrances and exits, new combinations, the solidarity of races . . ."

ALL FOUR: "Sail, sail thy best, ship of Democracy!" (*Join in last stanza of "America"*)
"Our fathers' God, to Thee,
Author of liberty,

To Thee we sing;
Long may our land be bright
With Freedom's holy light;
Protect us by Thy might,
Great God, our King." (*Curtain*)

THE . END

Sing the Songs of Pioneers

Characters

READER

TWO PILGRIMS

TWO CONTINENTALS

MORDECAI ⎫
NANCY   ⎬ *Pioneer scene in Kentucky*
MOTHER
MARY   ⎭

BEN   ⎫
SALLY   ⎬ *Pioneer scene in Ohio*
JOHN CHAPMAN ⎭

PREACHER

GEORGE   ⎫
JED   ⎪
PLAY-PARTY DANCERS ⎬ *Corn-husking scene*
HENRY   ⎪
BECKY   ⎭

TWO MEN   ⎫
TWO WOMEN ⎬ *Erie Canal scene*

CAPTAIN

SCHOOLBOY

Note: The words and music for the songs in this program may be found in *The Fireside Book of Favorite American Songs,* by Boni and Lloyd, Simon & Schuster, New York, 1952; *The Fireside Book of Folk Songs,* by Boni and Lloyd, Simon & Schuster, New York, 1947; *Singing Holidays,* by Oscar Brand, Knopf, New York, 1957.

TRUSTEE
HIS WIFE   } *Pioneer scene in Iowa*
DR. PITTS

BRIGHAM YOUNG
WILLIAM CLAYTON   } *On the way to Utah*

FORTY-NINERS
GOVERNMENT AGENT
BOY IN AUDIENCE

TIME: *The present.*

SETTING: *At one side of the stage are a few chairs, at the other side, a speaker's stand.*

AT RISE: *A medley of pioneer songs, either offstage singing, orchestra, or guitar music, precedes the opening of the play—such songs as "Oh, Susanna!", "Shuckin' of the Corn," "Green Grow the Lilacs," etc.*

The READER *comes in with book and goes to speaker's stand.*

READER: Pioneers! O pioneers!

From the beginning America has been a land of pioneers . . . defined by Webster as those "who go before, as into the wilderness, preparing the way for others to follow."

The Pilgrims seeking religious freedom almost 350 years ago were our first pioneers, willing to face starvation and danger and death for their faith. During that first cold New England winter more than half the colonists in Plymouth town died. At the meetinghouse those who remained lifted serious faces and sang hymns from *The Ainsworth Psalter,* which they brought with them from their temporary refuge in Holland.

(Spot on several PILGRIMS *who enter at other side of stage, holding hymn book. They sing "Pilgrim's Melody," and then exit.)*

All the early settlers were pioneers, venturing across the Atlantic to the new land, seeking a new life of freedom of one sort or another. With adventurous spirit men and women tore up their roots in the Old World and planted them confidently in the New. By the time of the Declaration of Independence, three million people had settled in the thirteen colonies along the Atlantic seaboard.

Then came the greatest pioneering feat of all in "preparing the way for others to follow" . . . the fight for independence and self-government. Yes, from the beginning America has been a country of pioneers!

(*Music of "Yankee Doodle" is heard from offstage. Two* CONTINENTALS *in tattered uniforms come into spot on side of stage.*)

1ST: Heard about the new way to spell America?

2ND: No, how?

1ST: In four letters.

2ND (*Counting on fingers*): A-M-E-R-I-C-A. That's seven.

1ST (*Counting on fingers*): F-R-E-E. That's four. And there couldn't be a better way to spell it. (*Begins to sing 1st stanza of "Free Amerikay."*)

"Torn from a world of tyrants,
Beneath this western sky,
We formed a new dominion,
A land of libertie . . ." (*Etc.*)

2ND (*Joining in on last line*): . . . "huzza for free Amerikay." (*Spot out,* CONTINENTALS *exit.*)

READER: But when we think of pioneers we usually do not think of the original settlers, or the soldiers who fought the Revolution. We think of those adventurous men and women who pressed westward, ever westward, from the thirteen colonies. We think of those who opened the wilderness by crossing rivers, climbing mountains, forcing their way through forests. ("*One More River*" *is heard from offstage—at first up, then down—as background.*)

Looking back at the long procession . . . from the end of the Revolution to the opening of the last public land in Indian Territory, Oklahoma, in 1893 . . . looking back and listening, our ears catch the essence of the pioneering spirit in the songs these people sang as they sought and conquered their promised lands. Listen! (*"Greenfields" is heard from offstage.*)

We are in a clearing in Kentucky, where a pioneer family has settled after pushing on from Virginia. In the cabin Mordecai Lincoln, the oldest son, is cleaning a long-rifle. Nancy is churning at an old-fashioned stomp churn, keeping time to her singing. The mother of the family sits and sews, while Mary, the youngest child, plays with a shabby doll.

(*During this exposition, family takes position at one side of stage. Spot up.*)

NANCY: How's it go again, Mammy? (*Sings from "Greenfields."*)

"Sweet prospects, sweet birds and sweet flow'rs
Have all lost their sweetness to me . . ."

What comes next?

MOTHER:

"The midsummer sun shines but dim,
The fields strive in vain to look gay;
But when I am happy in Him . . ."

NANCY: "December's as pleasant as May."

MOTHER (*Suddenly, looking around*): Mercy! Here we go singing the old songs and forgetting all about Tommy. Where's he gone, Nancy?

NANCY: I reckon he's around somewhere. I can't churn the butter and keep an eye on him at the same time, Mammy. Who'd think a six-year-old boy would need so much looking after!

MOTHER: I just hope he hasn't tried to follow Josiah to the fort.

MARY (*At door, looking out*): Tommy? Why, there he is in the clearing with Pappy.

MOTHER (*Looking*): So he is. They're out there a-planting together, putting in a crop. That'll keep Tommy out o' mischief for a bit. Mordecai, you'd best leave off cleaning that gun of your Pappy's and fetch a bucket o' water.

MORDECAI: Only one more minute and I'll fetch *two* buckets. Whyn't Josiah do it before toting the meal to the fort? Water's his job, hunting big game is mine.

NANCY: Doesn't he talk grown up, though! Just because he's turned fourteen.

MARY (*Crying out*): Mammy! Something flashed through the air . . . and Pappy's fallen over on the ground!

MOTHER (*Rushing to door*): Pappy? Reckon he stumbled on a root and hurt himself. (NANCY *and* MORDECAI *hurry to look, too,* MORDECAI *with the gun.*)

MARY: Mammy! Look . . . an Injun! He's making for Tommy.

MOTHER: No! No! (*Cries out*) Run, Tommy! Run for the fort!

NANCY: He's a-running, but so is the Injun. . . .

MORDECAI (*Raising gun*): Take that! (*There is a bang off-stage.*)

MOTHER: You hit him, Mordecai. He's staggering for the woods, holding his hands over his heart. Reckon he won't go far.

MORDECAI (*Reloading gun, ramming down powder*): I'm a-going to see if Pappy's all right and catch Tommy afore something worse happens.

MOTHER (*As* MORDECAI *hurries out*): You be careful, Mordecai. (*Spot out as* MOTHER, NANCY, *and* MARY *go out singing "O God, Our Help in Ages Past."*)

READER: Mordecai brought back a badly-scared Tommy

. . . but he couldn't bring back his father, the victim of an Indian arrow. Years later when the boy Tommy grew up and married a Kentucky girl, he named his son after his father, shot that day in the clearing. Named him Abraham. So young Abe and his grandfather had the self-same name . . . Abraham Lincoln!

Pioneers! O pioneers! No one will ever know how many fell before arrows shot by Indians who claimed the country as their own, by right of being there first. And no one will ever know how many settlers were crushed beneath falling trees as they tried to clear themselves a piece of land. Much of the wilderness in those days was covered with giant trees that shut out the sun. It took prodigious labor to carve out a home site, but the pioneers, undaunted, pitted their muscles and axes against the wilderness.

In the cabins women bent over smoky fireplaces to bake and keep the kettles bubbling; they spun and wove and made clothes; they churned and washed and rocked the cradle, and tried to keep a one-room cabin clean. More often than not they yearned for someone to talk to, for some sign of civilization. (*'The Juniper Tree' is heard from offstage—first up, then down as* READER *continues.*) Listen to what is happening in a one-room cabin on Licking Creek in Ohio, not far from the Ohio River. It is a morning in late October, 1801. Sally, still in her teens, is bending over a wooden wash tub when her young husband Ben comes in singing lustily. (*Spot on side of stage where* SALLY *is washing.* BEN *enters with axe.*)

BEN (*Singing "I Will Give My Love an Apple"*):
"I will give my love an apple without any core,
I will give my love a house without any door. . . ."

SALLY (*Interrupting*): But I would dearly love an apple *with* a core, Ben. 'Twas this time of year Papa's farm smelled of apples from one end to the other. I've not tasted one since we left Pennsylvania last spring. (*Sighs, then brightens*) And I'm glad our house has a door, even if it isn't very tight on its leather hinges! You'd best fix it before cold weather, Ben.

BEN (*Continuing his song*):
"I will give my love a palace wherein she may be,
And she may unlock it without any key."

SALLY (*Entering into spirit of song*):
"How *can* there be an apple without any core. . . ."
(*Etc.*)

BEN (*Answering*):
"My head is an apple without any core,
My mind is the house without any door . . ." (*Etc.*)
(*He takes her in his arms.*) Ah, Sally, my girl, there's a fine sight of fall outdoors this morning, a-glinting around the clearing, creeping up on the frost in the shadows."

SALLY (*Without looking up*): October's almost over. I dread to think of winter, Ben. 'Way off here. . . .

BEN: Winter? 'Twon't be so bad, Sal. I'll get a good bit of clearing done. Good chance to burn brush, too, after the snow falls, when there's no danger of the fire spreading. Brisk weather for a man to be felling trees. . . .

SALLY: And for a woman to be wishing for somebody to neighbor with. (*She catches herself.*) Oh, I'm sorry, Ben. I didn't mean for you to know. But I've been smelling fall in the air, too . . . and thinking of back home in Pennsylvania at apple-picking time.

BEN: Reckon most of them are picked already, and the cider mills busy as all get-out.

SALLY: Makes me a mite lonesome to think of it.

BEN: If there wasn't so much to do, I'd take you back for a visit, Sal. But 'twould set me back frightfully in my work.

SALLY: I know. I wouldn't be asking it. (*Sniffs, head up.*

Sniffs again.) Ben! Am I losing my mind? Seems I'm a-smelling apples . . . and not an apple tree growing for miles and miles. (*Sniffs*) Is it because I'm lonesome for Papa's old orchard and the settled look of his farm?

BEN (*Sniffing*): You've a better nose than I have, Sal . . . to smell windfalls.

SALLY (*Going to door to sniff again*): Ben! There's a stranger coming up the path from the creek! We've not had a visitor in weeks.

BEN (*Looking*): Young fellow, twenty-seven or twenty-eight, I'd say. Maybe he's figuring on taking up land somewhere near. (*Calls out*) Howdy!

JOHN CHAPMAN (*Coming in*): Howdy, folks. Pretty little clearing you've got here. I like the way it slopes to the south a mite. Mind if I stop and talk a bit? Name's John Chapman. I'm from Pennsylvania a few days back . . . floated down the Ohio in two canoes lashed together. Nudged up the creek here to look around.

SALLY (*Eagerly*): Looking for a place to settle?

CHAPMAN: Not me. No, I'm just looking for a few likely sites to plant a bit o' my dream.

BEN *and* SALLY (*Intrigued*): Your dream?

CHAPMAN: We all have our dreams. (*To* BEN) You, to conquer a piece of the wilderness. (*To* SALLY) You, to make a home, like the place you came from . . . or better. Me, my dream's different. I'm not the kind to marry and settle down. Yet I want my footprints to show, you might say, as I move through the wilds. I've a dream of apple trees.

SALLY: Apple trees! Do you hear, Ben? It's what I was talking about a while ago. Apple trees.

CHAPMAN: Apple trees here in Ohio. Seeds for nurslings . . . nurslings for orchards . . . an orchard for every settler pushing into this beautiful land. I've two canoes

full of decaying apples right now, from the cider presses
of western Pennsylvania.

SALLY: I knew I smelled apples!

CHAPMAN: Folks are beginning to call me Johnny Appleseed, from all the apple seeds I tote around. (*To* BEN)
Now if you could spare a bit of your south clearing, I'd
like to start a nursery, get some seedlings growing. You
can have your pick of the trees for your trouble.

SALLY: Oh, Ben. Apple trees . . . like back home in Pennsylvania!

BEN (*To* CHAPMAN): Come on, let's take a look. (*They go
out.* SALLY *dances around happily to the tune of "The
Juniper Tree" changing the words as she sings.*)

SALLY:

"Oh, sister Phoebe, how merry were we,
The night we sat under the appleseed tree,
The appleseed tree, hi-o, hi-o,
The appleseed tree, hi-o.

The apples were red and the leaves were green,
And the appleseed tree was the finest I've seen.
The appleseed tree. . . ." (*Etc.*)

READER (*As* SALLY *exits*): The pioneers faced danger, and
loneliness, and hard work, and discomfort. The typical
frontier cabin was a dark and crowded place. Here is the
way a circuit-riding preacher described one, on the basis
of first-hand experience after traveling a 300-mile circuit
to preach to a handful of families. He wrote a book about
it later . . . *The Pioneer Preacher,* by William Henry
Milburn. (*Spot on* PREACHER *at one side. He has a sense
of humor and gesticulates amusingly as he speaks.*)

PREACHER: The cabin is twelve by fourteen feet, and one
story high. The spaces between the logs are chinked and
then daubed with mud for plaster. The interior consists

of one room, one end of which is occupied by a fireplace. In this room are to sleep the man, his wife, the fifteen or twenty children bestowed upon him by Providence —and as the woods are full of "varmints," hens and chickens must be brought in for safekeeping, and as the dogs constitute an important portion of every hunter's family, they also take potluck with the rest. Possibly there may be another apartment in the cabin. You gain access to it by a rickety stepladder in one corner of the cabin. Toiling up this steep ascent you reach a loft, formed by laying loose clapboards on the rafters. . . . Your bed is a bearskin, a buffalo skin, or a tick filled with shucks. (*Spot out,* PREACHER *exits.*)

READER: Still, that pioneer cabin was home. (*Background music up on "Home, Sweet Home."*) And when "Home, Sweet Home" was published in 1823, it was an immediate success, spreading along the seaboard and catching up with the pioneers on the frontier. (*Music down.*)

Fortunately, pioneering wasn't all work and danger and privation and loneliness. Men and women had a way of turning some of their work into fun. They held log-rollings, and house-raisings, when settlers from miles around gathered to do a job . . . the men to handle the heavy work, the women to prepare a feast. They had quilting parties and corn-huskings. Listen! (*"The Shuckin' of the Corn" is heard from offstage. Spot on* GEORGE *and* JED *coming in at one side.*)

GEORGE (*Looking around furtively*): I've found two red ears, Jed. (*Takes them out of his pocket and shows them proudly.*) We've *got* to slip at least one of them where Henry's husking, so he'll shuck a red ear! He's moony over Becky Bolton, but too shy to look at her hardly.

JED: Never saw anybody so shy when it comes to girls.

GEORGE: If he shucks a red ear though . . . everybody knows you get to kiss a girl if you shuck a red ear!

JED: But if Henry's too shy to *look* at a girl, he's too shy to kiss her, red ear or not.

GEORGE: The rest of us'll have something to say about *that*. Honest, I think all Henry needs is a red ear to break the spell. We'll rush him into action before he has a chance to disappear. (*They hurry out. Music up again on "The Shuckin' of the Corn." A group of* BOYS *and* GIRLS *come in and play-party dance to the song as they sing and clap out all three stanzas. They exit. Spot on* HENRY *and* BECKY *coming in.*)

HENRY: Pleasures me to walk you home, Becky.

BECKY: Pleasures me to have you, Henry.

HENRY: Reckon if it hadn't been for that red ear and them a-pushing me on, I never *would* have screwed up my courage . . . to let you know I liked you. And I've liked you for a long time.

BECKY: I've been hoping you'd tell me.

HENRY: Seemed that red ear was fate pure and simple, Becky. (*Grins at her*) Want to know a secret? (*Takes ear of corn out of pocket*) I had a red ear in my pocket all the time, but durned if I wasn't too scared to slip it in the pile. 'Twas pure fate there was one in there already! (*Begins to sing last stanza of "Shuckin' of the Corn."*)

"The corn is red on the cornstalks,
The leaves are red on the tree,
And I'll be true to my true love,
If she will be true to me."

(BECKY *joins in chorus. They go out. Spot down.*)

READER: While pioneers were crossing the mountains into Tennessee or floating down the Ohio to find homes in Kentucky, Indiana, Illinois, and Missouri, Governor DeWitt Clinton and other New Yorkers were putting through plans for connecting the Hudson River with Lake Erie by canal, connecting Albany with Buffalo.

It took a while, of course, to build a canal 350 miles long, the longest canal in the world at that time. And it took a lot of money for those days . . . more than seven million dollars. But in 1825 the Erie Canal was opened for business. It immediately became a busy artery of travel and transport, a great new highway to the West.

Soon after the opening of the Canal, two young couples were up on the roof of the cabin of a canal boat, admiring the scenery on their first morning out from Albany. A pair of strong mules on the tow-path pulled the boat up the canal. (*Spot on* TWO WOMEN *and* TWO MEN *at side of stage, talking together.*)

1ST WOMAN (*To* 2ND): Isn't a canal boat wonderful? So much faster and more comfortable than going all the way by stage or wagon. I told my husband if he'd be willing to take the Canal as far as we could go, I'd be willing to travel the rest of the way by wagon.

2ND WOMAN: What I like is moving along both day and night. It shortens the journey so. (WOMEN *pantomime as* MEN *talk.*)

1ST MAN (*To* 2ND): From Buffalo we go the length of Lake Erie to Detroit, on one of those lake steamboats. Then by horse and wagon into southern Michigan. That country sounds good to me.

2ND MAN: We have relatives in Buffalo. Plan to stay there a while before deciding. Heard anything about that military road from Detroit to the tip of Lake Michigan?

1ST MAN: It's not finished yet by any means. (*Talk switches to* WOMEN)

1ST WOMAN: Yes, it's my first experience on a canal boat. I don't know how I'm going to like those narrow shelf beds to sleep on. (*Male voice offstage begins to sing "The Erie Canal."*) Listen! That mule-driver's beginning to sing.

2ND WOMAN: He probably gets lonesome. (CAPTAIN's *voice offstage, calling loudly.*)

CAPTAIN: Heed the hoggie, you folks up there! Heed the hoggie!

WOMEN: The hoggie?

1ST MAN: Wasn't that the captain?

CAPTAIN (*Hurrying in*): Heed the mule-driver, folks!

MULE-DRIVER (*Offstage, voice up*):

"Low bridge, ev'rybody down!

Low bridge, for we're comin' to a town."

CAPTAIN (*Excited*): Down! Down to the cabin, 'less you want to get your heads cracked on a bridge. Hurry! (*All rush out.*)

MULE-DRIVER:

"And you'll always know your neighbor,

You'll always know your pal,

If you've ever navigated on the Erie Canal. . . ." (*Etc.*)

READER: The pioneers had itching feet. As soon as the country around them began to fill up, many settlers pushed farther west where the forest was still untamed or the prairie unbroken. In December 1816, the man Tom Lincoln, who had named his son Abraham, moved his family from a Kentucky farm on the well-traveled road between Louisville and Nashville to sparsely-settled southern Indiana where the nearest doctor was thirty miles away. Fourteen years later he moved again, farther west, to central Illinois.

Westward, westward, in search of the Promised Land! The women tagged along, often reluctant to leave neighbors, schools, and meetinghouses behind. But the pioneering spirit kept them going. In their book the best was always ahead!

As soon as a few families were settled in a district, the womenfolk began to think of schools and churches.

Sometimes they dreamed for a good many years before their dreams came true. Their menfolk, burdened with the task of clearing land and growing crops and hunting, had little time to work on community buildings and little money for paying a teacher. Pioneers near Peach Bottom ferry on the Susquehanna in Pennsylvania were lucky when they found a huge hollow tree, big enough for a school room.

The typical pioneer school was a rough log cabin, with wind whistling through the cracks and cold coming up through the puncheon floor . . . if there was a floor. Books were few. That is the kind of school young Abe Lincoln went to "by littles." Although he went to four schools in all, one in Kentucky and three in Indiana, the sessions added up to only about a year altogether. Still it was better than no schooling at all, the fate of some children.

(*Spot on side of stage where* SCHOOLBOY *enters and acts out* "*Ha, Ha, Thisaway.*")

SCHOOLBOY (*Singing* 2ND *stanza*):

"I went into the school there, little old school there,
Went into the school there. . . . (*Etc.*)
Ha, ha, thisaway; (*Bends to left*)
Ha, ha, thataway; (*Bends to right*)
Ha, ha, thisaway (*Bends to left*)
Then, oh, then." (*Claps for each word*)

(SCHOOLBOY *exits after finishing song. Spot out.*)

READER: After a school, a church. In the absence of a meetinghouse, the circuit-riding preacher would hold services in one of his parishioner's cabins. But sooner or later the settlers would get together and build a community church.

Over in Iowa, for instance, a group of pioneers worked for almost five years to build their church, contributing all the labor and materials. When it finally was finished, just before Christmas, they decided to hold a dedication service. One evening a few days before the ceremony, the trustee in charge of the program was sitting quietly at home with his wife when they heard a knock on the door.

(*Spot on* TRUSTEE *and* WIFE *sitting at side of stage. Knock on door.*)

TRUSTEE: Come in, whoever ye be! (*Goes to door*) Why, Dr. Pitts, come in and warm yourself this cold night.

WIFE: Good evening, Doctor.

DR. PITTS: I've come about the church.

TRUSTEE (*Proudly*): All finished to the last plank and nail, Doctor, thanks to good workers such as yourself. We never knew a doctor to be so handy with a saw and hammer! And the dedication program is complete, too. We have reason to be proud, all of us.

WIFE: Do sit down, Doctor. Let me take your coat. (*Puts it on chair*)

DR. PITTS: About the dedication service. . . .

TRUSTEE: An address by the preacher, of course. Reports by some of the committees. A few appropriate hymns. . . .

WIFE: We have been practicing for weeks!

DR. PITTS (*Somewhat hesitant*): Would you . . . would you (*Takes paper from pocket and hands it to* TRUSTEE'S WIFE) . . . mind looking at this?

WIFE (*Taking paper*): Why, it's a song. "Little Brown Church in the Vale." What a lovely title . . . and so much like *our* little church in the vale. (*Hums tune*)

TRUSTEE: Sing it out, Nellie, so I can hear. Sing out the words.

WIFE (*Singing*):
"There's a church in the valley by the wildwood,
No lovelier place in the dale."

TRUSTEE: That's true of our church.

WIFE: "No spot is so dear to my childhood . . ." (*Looks up*) Oh, I hope our children will feel that way! "As the little brown church in the vale. Oh, come to the church in the wildwood. . ." (*Etc.*)

TRUSTEE (*Excited*): Why, you'd think the song was written especially for us . . . for the dedication program. Where did you find it, Doctor?

WIFE: It's lovely. *Where* did you get it?

DR. PITTS: I . . . I wrote it.

TRUSTEE *and* WIFE: You *did!*

WIFE (*To* HUSBAND): You must go round up the choir. I can't *wait* to hear them sing it. Come with me to the church so you can hear it on the new organ . . .

(*Spot out,* TRUSTEE, WIFE, *and* DR. PITTS *exit.*)

READER: Dr. Pitts' song became famous, and so did the little brown church in the vale built by Iowa pioneers. Tourists still stop to visit it.

Even before Dr. Pitts wrote his song, another religious song played its part in pioneer history. Five years after the opening of the Erie Canal, a group of Mormons, under the leadership of Joseph Smith, left New York in search of their Promised Land. First they tried living in Ohio, then in Missouri, then in Illinois. Finally, in 1847, with Brigham Young in charge, they crossed the Missouri River and headed for the desert and Great Salt Lake, where they hoped they could live and work and worship as they pleased, without interference. The long trip by covered wagon was grueling and dangerous, and the Mormons were burdened with troubles. Even the great faith and energy of their leader Brigham Young was often sorely tried.

One evening in late spring the group was camping for the night on the west side of the Rockies, after a particularly trying day. Brigham Young sat brooding by the campfire when William Clayton took a seat beside him.

(Spot on YOUNG *as* CLAYTON *comes in and sits down beside him.)*

CLAYTON: We can give thanks that nothing disastrous happened when we crossed that rushing stream this afternoon.

YOUNG: Aye, that we can, Brother William.

CLAYTON: Our wagons are so heavily loaded, they tip easily. Only the hand of the Lord saved us from losing some of our equipment today.

YOUNG: "Behold, the Lord's hand is not shortened, that it cannot save." Yet even with the Lord on our side, I sometimes doubt our wisdom in trying to carry so much over the mountains and across the desert . . . plows, implements, seed grain, a year's supply of provisions. The mules and oxen can be pushed only so far. And what barriers we have to cross!

CLAYTON: Ah, but they will be barriers for intruders, too.

YOUNG: You are right. The place we have chosen is so remote, so barren and uninviting, surely no one else will think of it as a land of promise. But we shall water the desert and make it bloom like a rose!

CLAYTON: And so we should be going with joy, instead of being burdened with troubles. We should lift our faces and sing along the way!

YOUNG: Aye.

CLAYTON: I was thinking today as I walked beside the oxen that a good spirited song would help us forget our difficulties, would help turn these mountains into molehills. And even as I thought, the words and music of a new song came to me full-blown, you might say.

YOUNG *(Eagerly)*: A new song!

CLAYTON: I have called it "Come, Come, Ye Saints."

YOUNG *(Standing)*: You must sing it for us. *(Calls out)* Come, come, ye Saints! Come, come. Brother William has a new song for us!

CLAYTON (*Singing first two stanzas*):
   "Come, come, ye Saints, no toil nor labor fear,
   But with joy wend your way. . . ." (*Etc.*)

YOUNG (*Enthusiastically*): You must sing it again and teach
   us the words. Tomorrow we shall cross the mountains,
   singing!

(*Spot out as* CLAYTON *and* YOUNG *exit to the music.*)

READER: That song William Clayton thought of on the
   way to Utah became the official Mormon hymn.

   The pioneers pushed on.

   More and more of them ventured across the Missouri
   River, crossed the plains to the Rockies, crossed the
   Rockies to the Pacific. In 1843 the great migration to
   Oregon began . . . with a large party of a thousand
   men, women and children, 120 wagons drawn by oxen,
   and several thousand horses and cows.

   By 1846 settlers were delighting in the fertile soil and
   mild climate of California. Then, three years later, came
   the discovery of gold in the Sacramento Valley, and the
   gold rush began! Within two years a hundred thousand
   immigrants poured into the gold regions of California.

   They came by sailing vessel around Cape Horn or
   crossed the Isthmus of Panama, singing "Sacramento."

(*Spot on* FORTY-NINERS *singing as they cross the stage.*)

FORTY-NINERS:
   "A bully ship and a bully crew, Doo-da, doo-da!
   A bully mate and a captain too. . . ." (*Etc.*)

READER: And they came by overland trail across the desert,
   across the mountains, singing "Sweet Betsy from Pike"
   and "Oh, Susanna!" . . . both great favorites with the
   forty-niners. (*Spot on two more* FORTY-NINERS *coming
   in*).

1ST: I say *Betsy*.

2ND: I say *Susanna*.

1ST (*Taking out coin*): Heads or tails?

2ND: Heads.

1ST (*Flipping coin; both look*): Heads. All right, let's go. (*They sing "Oh, Susanna" as they cross the stage.*)

READER: The country was filling up. Out on the plains, land was cheap and railroads were beginning to make it more accessible. The government held the price down to encourage settlement. And then in 1862 the Homestead Act was passed. Government agents went around drumming up business, painting a rosy picture of free land out West. From Scandinavia and other north-European countries, immigrants swarmed in by the thousands. Uncle Sam had his arms wide open, and his agents sang out convincingly: "Come along, come along . . . we have room for all creation and our banner is unfurled." (*Spot on side of stage.* GOVERNMENT AGENT *comes in, addresses audience.*)

AGENT: Settle out West, my friends, out on the rolling plains. Out where opportunity stretches as far as the horizon! In what other country in the world can you match the offer Uncle Sam makes under the Homestead Act? Any one of you . . . any one who is head of a family or twenty-one years old . . . man or woman . . . can enter a claim to 160 acres of land! Think of it. Any one of you . . . whether already a citizen or intending to take out your papers . . . can occupy the land for five years, build a house and do some planting, and it's yours . . . *yours,* my friends, fully and forever. (*He swings into "Uncle Sam's Farm"*)

"Of all the mighty nations in the east and in the west, Our glorious Yankee nation is the greatest and the best. . . ." (*Etc.*)

(*Spot out at end of song.* AGENT *exits.*)

READER: The time came, of course, when our open spaces were no more. Dissatisfied settlers could no longer pull up stakes and file on a homestead farther west. The age of the pioneer was over . . . the chapter closed. . . .

BOY (*Standing in audience*): Closed? Wait a minute. I object. The chapter is far from closed.

READER (*Somewhat taken aback*): Where can you get cheap government land today? Where can you homestead a quarter section?

BOY (*Going up to stage*): Let's go back to your definition of a pioneer. What was it again?

READER (*Turning back*): "One who goes before, as into the wilderness, preparing the way for others to follow." (*Looks up*) But there is no wilderness left, not in the United States. No more rivers to cross, no more frontiers to conquer. Unless you're thinking about outer space . . . rockets to the moon and the planets. But you must admit that's out for most of us.

BOY: I'm not thinking of outer space. I'm thinking of down-to-earth frontiers all around us.

READER: What frontiers?

BOY: The Peace Corps has the right idea. Frontiers of brotherhood . . . peace . . . understanding.

READER: But you must have something to put your finger on, not just words.

BOY: I know. But you can put your finger on something besides *land*. What was that you said back at the beginning . . . about our kind of government being such a great pioneering feat? Maybe that isn't the common conception of pioneering . . . but it certainly was preparing a wonderful way for others to follow.

READER: Well. . . .

BOY: You know what I think? I think history will show that some of our greatest pioneers, in the most far-reaching sense, belong to the twentieth century, to the present day. Why, I've just been reading about a man who has been pioneering in sixty different countries.

READER: Sixty countries!

Boy: His wilderness happens to be the field of illiteracy—
a harder field to plow than prairie sod ever was. His
name is Frank Laubach . . . and he's helped eighty
million people to learn to read! You must have heard
of his "Each one teach one" program.

Reader: Yes. But I never thought of it as pioneering.

Boy: But why not? What kind of pioneering could be more
exciting? And there's Clifford Clifton out in Los Angeles
who started Meals for Millions . . . to supply cheap
but nourishing meals for hungry people overseas, millions of them. Those are two modern pioneers I can
think of offhand. Pioneering is in our blood, it's in our
heritage. We can't stop just because there aren't any
more homesteads!

Reader: Well, if you put it that way. . . .

Boy: We can't stop and we don't want to! Nations that stop
pioneering, stop growing—that's common knowledge.
It's up to us (*Spreads arms to include audience*) to keep
preparing the way for others to follow. The good way.
We don't want to sit down in twentieth-century comfort and grow soft. For a country with pioneering in its
heritage, there's *always* one more river to cross, and we
can thank God there is. (*Music for "One More River"
is heard.*) Let's go! (*Begins to sing*)
"Old Noah he built the Ark" (*Gestures to audience to
sing*)

All: "There's one more river to cross."

Boy: "And he patched it up with hickory bark,"

All (*Changing Chorus somewhat*):
"There's one more river to cross.
One more river, and that's the river before us,
One more river,
A river ever to cross."

THE END

Sing the Songs of Thanksgiving

Characters

MASTER OF CEREMONIES	WILLIAM BRADFORD
WILLIAM BREWSTER	SUSANNA WINSLOW
EDWARD WINSLOW	3 WOMEN
ELIZABETH WINSLOW	BOYS
GIRL	GIRLS } *chorus*
BOY	

TIME: *The present.*

SETTING: *Stage is decorated to suggest the harvest season, with shocks of corn or grain at either side. There are two rustic benches at left. Stand for* MASTER OF CEREMONIES *is up front at right.*

AT RISE: CHORUS *comes in from both sides carrying baskets of fruit, ears of corn, pumpkins, and other bounty of the harvest. They are singing the first stanza of "Come, Ye Thankful People, Come," and as they sing they place the fruits of the harvest in front of the corn shocks. At the end of the stanza* BOYS *and* GIRLS *call out:*

BOYS:

"Singing the reapers homeward come, Io! Io!"

Note: With the exception of "Over the River and Through the Wood," which is in most school music books, the songs in this play can be found in these two books: *A Treasury of Hymns,* Simon and Schuster, New York, 1953; and *The Family Book of Favorite Hymns,* Funk & Wagnalls Co., New York, 1950.

GIRLS:
"Merrily singing the harvest home, Io! Io!"

BOYS:
"Along the fields, along the road,
Where autumn is scattering leaves abroad,
Homeward cometh the ripe last load, Io! Io!" (CHORUS *groups itself near back of stage and goes into second stanza of "Come, Ye Thankful People, Come."*)

CHORUS: "All the world is God's own field . . ." (*Etc.*) (MASTER OF CEREMONIES *enters toward end of stanza and takes place at reading stand.*)

M.C.: "Come, ye thankful people, come, raise the song of harvest home." In other words, sing the songs of Thanksgiving! For this, my friends, is the season when man expresses his gratitude for the blessings he has received. This is the time for feasting and sharing, for looking back over the year and seeing that it was good. This is the time for giving thanks to that all-embracing power that runs the universe.

CHORUS (*Softly*):
"All is safely gathered in
Ere the winter storms begin."

M.C.: The idea is as old as civilization. No one really knows when or where men first thought of setting aside time for a feast of thanksgiving. The custom is there—as far back as the records go. Centuries before the birth of Christ, the Hebrews held their Feast of the Tabernacles at the time of the full moon of the harvest month, to celebrate the ingathering of crops.

1ST BOY IN CHORUS: "Thou shalt keep the feast of harvest: the first fruits of thy labours, which thou hast sown in the field, and the feast of ingathering, which is in the end of the year, when thou hast gathered in thy labours out of the field."

M.C.: The Feast of the Tabernacles was a joyous week,

celebrated mostly in specially built booths or little huts made of branches, leaves, and flowers. The little huts were set up in yards or on the flat roofs of the houses, in memory of the way the wandering tribes of Israel had lived in the wilderness during their long search for the promised land.

2ND BOY: "When ye have gathered in the fruit of the land, ye shall keep a feast unto the Lord seven days . . . and ye shall take . . . the boughs of goodly trees . . . and ye shall dwell in booths seven days."

3RD BOY: "And thou shalt rejoice in thy feast, thou, and thy son, and thy daughter . . . the stranger, and the fatherless, and the widow, that are within thy gates."

CHORUS (*From "Come, Ye Thankful People, Come"*):
"God, our Maker, doth provide
For our wants to be supplied:
Come to God's own temple, come,
Raise the song of harvest home."

M.C.: Some famous old psalms of thanksgiving are included in the book of Psalms in the Old Testament. At least two of them, the 65th and the 67th, were composed many years before the birth of Christ as special songs for the great harvest festival. The tunes have been lost in the ages, but the words still ring out loud and clear:

BOYS: "Praise waiteth for thee, O God . . . thou makest the outgoings of the morning and evening to rejoice."

GIRLS: "Thou crownest the year with thy goodness; and thy paths drop fatness."

BOYS: "They drop upon the pastures of the wilderness and the little hills rejoice on every side."

GIRLS: "The pastures are clothed with flocks; the valleys also are covered over with corn . . ."

BOYS *and* GIRLS: "O let the nations be glad and sing for joy . . . let the people praise thee, O God; let all the people praise thee."

M.C.: All over the ancient world there was rejoicing for the harvest. The Greeks held an annual late-fall festival in honor of Demeter, goddess of agriculture. Her symbols were ears of corn, the poppy, and the mystic basket of flowers, corn, and fruits. In Rome, the Greek Demeter became Ceres, from whom we get our word *cereal*. Ceres, Roman goddess of crops, was honored with a festival at harvest time.

CHORUS:

"First the blade, and then the ear,

Then the full corn shall appear."

M.C.: Over the centuries the custom of holding harvest festivals spread across Europe. In medieval times the most common thanksgiving celebration was held on November 11, Saint Martin's Day. In France, Germany, Holland, England, and countries of central Europe this day was a holiday, with Saint Martin's goose and Saint Martin's wine on the festive table.

CHORUS:

"God, our Maker, doth provide

For our wants to be supplied."

M.C.: Many tribes of American Indians celebrated harvest festivals long before the Pilgrims landed on our shores. Is it any wonder that hymns of thanksgiving have been popular down the years? Is it any wonder that so many people all over the world still sing to the Lord of the Harvest? (CHORUS *swings into "Sing to the Lord of Harvest," singing at least the first stanza and the one beginning "By Him the clouds drop fatness." As they near the end of the final stanza,* WILLIAM BREWSTER, EDWARD WINSLOW *and* ELIZABETH WINSLOW *come in from left and sit on the benches.*) Now let us stop briefly at a point in time which has a direct bearing on our own observance of Thanksgiving here in the United States: The year is 1619. The place is Leyden, Holland. A number of peace-loving Englishmen, who were denied freedom of worship in their homeland, escaped to Holland and have now been living in Leyden for about ten years. William Brewster, Elder of the group, is owner of a print shop. Late one autumn afternoon we find Elder Brewster talking to his young assistant Edward Winslow and to Edward's wife Elizabeth:

BREWSTER: There's nothing for me to do but close the print shop, Edward. It would be dangerous for us to keep on, under the circumstances.

EDWARD: But what if King James *is* offended by that book you published, sir? What can he do to you here in Holland?

BREWSTER: It's not just that the book offends the King of England. If the matter stopped there, I, too, should say, "What of it?" But word came this morning that the English government is complaining to the Dutch authorities about it. That bodes no good. I'm sorry, Edward. I have decided that the best course is to close the shop, lest our Separatist group here get into trouble. I shall speak to William Bradford about finding a place for you in his weaving business, if nothing turns up in the printing line.

ELIZABETH: But what about you, Elder Brewster? What will you do when the shop is closed?

BREWSTER: I think I shall take my family back to England.

EDWARD *and* ELIZABETH: To England!

BREWSTER: I'll probably be as safe there as I am here now. And it won't be for long, you know. Our plans for sailing to the New World are almost complete. For two years we have been planning the undertaking; next year we hope to sail. So I shall not be long in England.

ELIZABETH: Edward is eager to go to the New World, but I am not so sure.

BREWSTER: There will be hardships, of course. No one will deny it. But we will be free to live our lives as we wish.

ELIZABETH: We have religious freedom here in Holland, haven't we, Elder Brewster? And things are so pleasant. Like us, the Dutch are a peace-loving people, and so kind.

BREWSTER: True, Elizabeth, but you are young. You and Edward have been married only a year. You do not have a family growing up amidst strange customs.

ELIZABETH: But can't we keep our own ways and customs here in Leyden?

BREWSTER: It is not easy. I have been in Holland eleven years now. Can I keep my children from having Dutch friends and learning Dutch ways and adopting Dutch ideas? No. It is impossible. And not right, either, to keep them apart. (*Offstage, children are heard singing "We Gather Together."*) The children are coming home from school.

ELIZABETH: They're singing the Dutch hymn of thanksgiving, "We Gather Together." (*Rises, looks toward wings*) It's a beautiful hymn, I think. Oh, I see two of our Separatist children in the group!

BREWSTER (*Hurrying to look*): Yes. And that's just what I mean, Mistress Winslow. Our English children are bound to turn into little Hollanders if we stay here. Wait, I'll call them. (*Exits*)

ELIZABETH (*Turning to* EDWARD): Perhaps I shouldn't have expressed my doubts about the new colony, Edward. I'm sorry. But I have a feeling of foreboding I can't seem to shake off. Yet, in the depth of my heart, wherever you want to go, I want to go. You know that.

EDWARD: Think of the adventure it will be! What an opportunity! I'll take care of you, Elizabeth. Don't be afraid. (BREWSTER *enters with* BOY *and* GIRL.)

BREWSTER: I want you to sing it for the Winslows, children.

GIRL: But doesn't everybody know it already, Elder Brewster?

BREWSTER: Come, let's hear how it goes. (BOY *and* GIRL *sing three stanzas of "We Gather Together."*)

ELIZABETH (*Enthusiastically, as they finish*): It's a beautiful hymn of thanksgiving. I know most of the words myself.

BREWSTER: Yes, but have you thought what the words mean, Mistress Winslow? They're not what we English expect in a hymn of thanksgiving. Most of our thanksgiving songs have to do with the ingathering of the harvest. But these words! "The wicked oppressing now cease from distressing." And "So from the beginning the fight we are winning." What do they mean to us as Englishmen?

BOY: I know what they mean. We won the war against Spain forty or fifty years ago. This is a song of thanksgiving for that victory.

BREWSTER: *We* won the war?

GIRL: The Spaniards tried to rule us but we rebelled.

BOY: There was a long fight, but the Dutch finally declared their independence, in 1581. No wonder there's a thanksgiving hymn about it.

BREWSTER (*To* ELIZABETH): You see? *We* won the war. *We* rebelled. Eleven years in Holland, and our children are no longer English! It is time we were founding an English colony of our own in the New World.

ELIZABETH: Well, anyway, it's a beautiful hymn, Elder Brewster. We must take it along with us to America, to sing on our own Thanksgiving Day in the land of freedom! (*As they go out,* CHORUS *sings last stanza of "We Gather Together."*)

M.C.: The following year, in September, 1620, the *Mayflower* set sail from Plymouth, England, with 102 passengers—men, women, and children, bound for America.

BOY IN CHORUS (*Eagerly*): Everyone knows what comes next!

M.C.: What comes next?

BOY: The landing of the Pilgrim fathers on Plymouth Rock. It was a cold, gray New England day. "The breaking waves dashed high . . ." (CHORUS *swings into "The Breaking Waves Dashed High," also known as "The Landing of the Pilgrim Fathers." They sing three or four stanzas, including the one beginning "What sought they thus afar?"*)

M.C.: That's a very nice song, but it really isn't a Thanksgiving song, you know.

GIRL: Not a Thanksgiving song? It's about the Pilgrims.

M.C.: But there isn't a word of thanksgiving in it. It's really a Forefather's Day song, a song for December 22, to commemorate the landing at Plymouth. But I will admit it gets into most Thanksgiving programs, and no one seems to mind. "What sought they thus afar? Bright jewels of the mine? The wealth of seas, the spoils of war?"

CHORUS: "They sought a faith's pure shrine."

M.C.: Yes, the Pilgrims sought a faith's pure shrine. But the hardships they endured were almost overwhelming. That first year at Plymouth, forty-six of the little band died—among them Edward Winslow's young wife, Elizabeth. Forty-six shallow graves were left unmarked on the hill, to keep the Indians from knowing how much the colony had dwindled.

CHORUS (*From "The Breaking Waves Dashed High"*):
"Ay, call it holy ground,
The soil where first they trod!
They have left unstained what there they found—
Freedom to worship God!"

M.C.: The winter was cold, houses few, food scarce. At one time only seven of the colonists were well enough

to work. Yet at the end of the first year, William Bradford, young governor of Plymouth, whose wife's grave
was on the hill near Elizabeth Winslow's, decided that
the colony's blessings warranted a day of thanksgiving.
(BRADFORD *and* BREWSTER *enter, sit on bench.*) It is late
fall, 1621. Governor Bradford is talking over plans with
Elder Brewster:

BRADFORD: You don't think it premature, then?

BREWSTER: In my opinion, taking time to give thanks is
never premature. The whole colony is in favor of your
idea for a Thanksgiving feast, Brother William.

BRADFORD: We have much to be grateful for. True, the
peas and barley and wheat didn't amount to much,
but our twenty acres of Indian corn yielded surpris-
ingly well. I have never heard of such a yield in England.

BREWSTER: We can thank Squanto for telling us to put
those three herrings in every hole for fertilizer.

BRADFORD: There's enough for a peck of corn and a peck
of meal for every person every week until the next harvest! That's double the rations we had last year.

BREWSTER: May last winter never be repeated!

BRADFORD: Eleven buildings in the colony now, and more
in the making; when we came there was nothing but
a desolate wilderness full of wild beasts and Indians.
What a blessing we were able to make friends with the
Indians!

BREWSTER: Ah, that reminds me, Brother William. A feast
of thanksgiving is something our Indian friends can
understand and appreciate. Why not invite Chief Massasoit and some of his braves to share with us?

BRADFORD: Why not, indeed! A few guests at the feast
should not tax the women too greatly, though there
are only five women left in the colony to do all the cooking and baking. By the way, Susanna Winslow is com-

ing in a moment to talk to me about the Thanksgiving singing. We can ask her what she thinks.

BREWSTER: What a feast it will be! Ah, venison, roast goose, roast duck, maybe even some of those long-legged wild turkeys.

BRADFORD: Lobsters, clams, eels, oysters—and all to be had for the taking.

BREWSTER: Watercress and leeks and herbs for salad.

BRADFORD: Corn bread, barley bread—

BREWSTER: And for dessert those wild plums and berries the women and children dried.

BRADFORD: All washed down with our good red and white wine from the wild grapes. Ah! (SUSANNA WINSLOW *enters.*)

SUSANNA: Good afternoon, gentlemen.

BRADFORD *and* BREWSTER: Peace be with you, Mistress Winslow.

SUSANNA: About the songs for the festival—do you have a moment to listen? I trained some of the children to sing, "All People That on Earth Do Dwell."

BREWSTER (*Nodding*): "Sing to the Lord with cheerful voice."

SUSANNA: Elder Brewster, your two sons—Love and Wrestling—and the Allerton children—Bartholomew, Remember, and Mary—do quite well together, and I thought it would be nice to have them sing at the festival. Will you hear them and say if you agree?

BREWSTER *and* BRADFORD: By all means, Mistress Winslow. (SUSANNA *beckons to three* BOYS *and two* GIRLS *in* CHORUS. *They step forward and, with* SUSANNA *directing, sing* a cappella *two or three stanzas of "All People That on Earth Do Dwell." At the end of the song,* BOYS *and* GIRLS *return to their places, and* SUSANNA *looks inquiringly at* BREWSTER *and* BRADFORD.)

SUSANNA: What do you think, gentlemen?

BRADFORD: Very good, indeed, Mistress Winslow.

BREWSTER: The song will add greatly to the celebration.

SUSANNA: There is one other thing I wish to speak to you about. You remember my husband's first wife Elizabeth—

BREWSTER: May the Lord bless her courageous soul. We all loved her.

BRADFORD: A fine young woman.

SUSANNA: The other day Edward was telling me about something that happened in Leyden. You were discussing with Edward and Elizabeth your decision to close the print shop, Elder Brewster, when you heard schoolchildren singing out in the street.

BREWSTER: I remember. Two of our Separatist children were in the group, singing a Dutch song.

SUSANNA (*Nodding*): "We Gather Together." And Elizabeth said: "We must take it along with us to America, to sing at our own Thanksgiving Day in the land of freedom."

BREWSTER: Yes.

SUSANNA: So I suggest we sing "We Gather Together" at the beginning and end of the festival in memory of all the brave ones who lie there on the hill.

BRADFORD: Thank you for the suggestion, Mistress Winslow. It shall be done!

BREWSTER (*Thoughtfully*): The words have more meaning now. "So, from the beginning, the fight we were winning." Slowly but surely we have been winning our fight for freedom!

BRADFORD (*To* SUSANNA): And now we have something to ask *you*. Elder Brewster has suggested that we invite a few of our Indian friends to celebrate Thanksgiving with us—Massasoit and some of his braves. Would that overtax the women in preparing the feast?

SUSANNA: A few more at the long tables? Oh, no, it

wouldn't be any trouble at all. The Indians have been good to us.

BRADFORD: Then I'll send a messenger to Massasoit immediately. Tell the women to count on preparing food for, say, a score extra. (*They go out.* CHORUS *softly repeats last stanza of "We Gather Together."*)

M.C.: Massasoit and a few of his braves were invited, but *ninety* came with their chief. Ninety-one Indians and fifty-five Pilgrims! The women were no doubt dismayed, but the whole colony rose to the occasion and welcomed their guests with friendship and good will. Fortunately, an Indian hunting party went out and brought back five deer for the feast. For three days the Pilgrims and their guests feasted and prayed and sang and played games and engaged in feats of skill and turned the meat spits over the fires. That first Thanksgiving in 1621 was a great success, even though it drew so heavily on the colony's reserve stock of provisions that rations had to be reduced for the second winter in Plymouth. The next fall, because of a poor harvest, no Thanksgiving feast was held. But in 1623 the Pilgrims celebrated again, and from then on the Thanksgiving custom spread slowly to other colonies.

GIRL: First Thanksgiving in Boston, 1630.

BOY: In the rest of the Massachusetts Bay Colony, 1632.

GIRL: First Thanksgiving in Connecticut, 1639.

BOY: First "Thanks Day" on Manhattan Island, New York, celebrated by the Dutch in 1644.

M.C.: Even in those early times, Thursday seems to have been the favored day, though the month of the year varied. By the time of the Revolutionary War the custom of an autumn Thanksgiving on Thursday was fairly well established. In spite of the terrible hardships facing our ragged Continentals, General Washington proclaimed a Thanksgiving at Valley Forge in 1777. When the war finally ended, the colonists were so grateful that they observed a special Thanksgiving Day. And in 1789, 168 years after the Pilgrims' first Thanksgiving, President Washington issued the first Thanksgiving Proclamation for the new United States of America.

BOY: "Now therefore I do recommend and assign Thursday the twenty-sixth day of November next to be devoted by the People of these States to the service of that great and glorious Being . . . That we may then all unite in rendering unto Him our sincere and humble thanks for His kind care and protection of the People of this country . . . for the great tranquility, union, and plenty, which we have enjoyed . . . and in general for all the great and various favors which He hath been pleased to confer upon us."

CHORUS (*From "Sing to the Lord of Harvest"*):
"He filleth with His fulness
All things with large increase;
He crowns the year with goodness,
With plenty and with peace."

M.C.: President Washington waited six years to proclaim another day of national thanksgiving. And after that, it wasn't long before presidential proclamations were few and far between. The practice reverted to a local or state basis. Some Thanksgivings were held in October, some in November, some on the first Thursday after the cattle were driven home from the common pasture. In a few states Thanksgiving was not observed at all. By 1800, Americans were adding a new song to their list of Thanksgiving favorites—a harvest song from Germany. Up to this time most of the songs had come from England or Holland. Now a song from the German countryside, "We Plow the Fields and Scatter," made a strong appeal to Americans, young and old. (CHORUS *sings first and last stanzas of "We Plow the Fields and Scat-*

ter.") And now we come to two nineteenth-century American women who played leading roles in making our Thanksgiving what it is today. One woman was from Massachusetts, the other from New Hampshire. Both lived at about the same time, both were well-known writers, and both were ardent crusaders. The first, Lydia Maria Child, started a children's magazine in 1826, when she was twenty-four years old. Out of her interest in children came Mrs. Child's Thanksgiving poem which has been spoken and sung by generations of American schoolchildren, and is still a favorite. (CHORUS *gaily goes into "Thanksgiving Day," more popularly called "Over the River and Through the Wood." They sing the entire song.*) The other woman was Sarah Josepha Hale of New Hampshire. At the time Mrs. Child started her children's magazine, Mrs. Hale was thirty-eight years old, a widow with five small children to support. She was trying to make a living by writing. At first she wrote verse, then a novel about New England. In this book there appeared an inkling of what was later to turn into a persistent campaign for a national Thanksgiving Day. Let us go back to a day several months after the publication of Mrs. Hale's novel. The year is 1828. Two Newport, New Hampshire, women are discussing it. (*Two* WOMEN *enter from left.* 1ST WOMAN *carries a book.*)

1ST WOMAN: Have you finished Mrs. Hale's book yet, Abigail?

2ND WOMAN: Goodness, no. I'm a slow reader, and besides, I want to make it last. I do think it's lovely.

1ST WOMAN: She has so many interesting ideas. This, for instance. (*Opens book and reads*) "We have too few holidays." I agree, don't you? "Thanksgiving, like the Fourth of July, should be considered a national festival observed by all our people." I think she's right.

2ND WOMAN: But we do observe Thanksgiving!

1ST WOMAN: Yes, here in New Hampshire. But it's so haphazard the country over. Some states don't celebrate it at all. (3RD WOMAN *comes hurrying in.*)

3RD WOMAN (*Calling out*): My dears, have you heard the news about Sarah Hale?

1ST WOMAN: Something new about her book?

3RD WOMAN: No, no. The letter.

1ST *and* 2ND WOMAN: What letter?

3RD WOMAN: Oh, it's so exciting. (*Confidentially*) Mrs. Hale has just had a letter from a gentleman in Boston. He was attracted by her novel. And he's asked her to become editor of a new magazine he's starting for women. Imagine!

1ST WOMAN: Will she do it?

3RD WOMAN: Of course, she'll do it. And if you ask me Sarah Hale will make a big splash in the literary pool.

M.C.: And so Sarah Josepha Hale became editor of the *Ladies' Magazine,* later *Godey's Lady's Book,* and began a fifty-year career as a writer and crusading editor. One of her crusades was a long and ardent one to get one day of the year set aside as a day of national thanksgiving— one day for everyone in the United States to celebrate together.

CHORUS:
"We seem to go
Extremely slow—
It is so hard to wait!"

M.C.: From 1846 on, Mrs. Hale bombarded presidents, governors and influential people everywhere with pleas to join in establishing a national day of Thanksgiving. She suggested the last Thursday in November, which had been President Washington's choice in his first Thanksgiving Proclamation. In 1852 she was able to report:

GIRL: "Last year 29 states and all territories united in the festival. This year we trust that Virginia and Vermont will come into the arrangement. . . . Twenty-three millions of people sitting down, as it were, together to a feast of joy and thankfulness."

CHORUS:
"Over the river and through the wood,
Now Grandmother's cap I spy!
Hurrah for the fun!
Is the pudding done?
Hurrah for the pumpkin pie!"

M.C.: In her zeal Mrs. Hale wrote literally thousands of letters by hand, to say nothing of countless editorials in *Godey's Lady's Book* promoting a national Thanksgiving Day. Then came the Civil War. But her crusade did not stop. Finally, in 1863, President Lincoln signed a proclamation:

BOY: "The year that is drawing to a close has been filled with the blessings of fruitful fields and healthful skies. . . . In the midst of a civil war of unequalled magnitude and severity . . . peace has been preserved with all nations, order has been maintained. . . . I do, therefore, invite my fellow citizens in every part of the United States . . . to set apart and observe the last Thursday of November next as a day of thanksgiving and praise. . . ."

M.C.: Sarah Josepha Hale had won her fight! From 1863 on, every President of the United States has proclaimed a Thursday in November as Thanksgiving Day. And so we come to the present, and to a Thanksgiving song which happily combines both the past and the present. We come to a song called "For the Summer's Glowing Pageant," with its old-world tune and twentieth-century words. The song celebrates the harvest season and at the same time injects a new note, a note of far-reaching brotherhood and good will. It ends with a prayer that our country, with roots in justice, and a heritage of hope, will bless all mankind. And so we sing of Thanksgiving for a new day! (CHORUS *sings first and third stanzas of* "For the Summer's Glowing Pageant.")

THE END

Sing the Songs of Christmas

Characters

MASTER OF CEREMONIES	LUTHER'S SONS
PEASANT	LUTHER'S DAUGHTER
2 WOODCARVERS	WAITS, *roving singers*
APPRENTICE WOODCARVER	3 INDIAN BRAVES
FRANCIS OF ASSISI	3 INDIAN CHIEFS
3 SHEPHERDS	ISAAC WATTS
JEANETTE	JOSEPH MOHR
ISABELLA	FRANZ GRUBER
CHILDREN	PHILLIPS BROOKS
MARTIN LUTHER	LEWIS REDNER
CATHERINE LUTHER	CHORUS

SETTING: *The stage is decorated gaily for Christmas.*

AT RISE: *The* CHORUS *stands upstage.* MASTER OF CERE- MONIES *comes in briskly, carrying a script, and goes to a reading stand at one side.*

M.C. (*To audience*): Merry Christmas! (*To* CHORUS) Merry Christmas!

BOY IN CHORUS: In French it's Joyeux Noël.

GIRL: In China it's Tin Hao Nian.

BOY: In Italy it's Buon Natale.

Note: Words and music to the carols in this program may be found in *A Treasury of Christmas Songs and Carols,* edited by Henry W. Simon, Houghton Mifflin, Boston, 1955; or in *Fireside Book of Folk Songs,* edited by Boni, Lloyd, and Provensen, Simon & Schuster, New York, 1947.

GIRL: In Germany it's Froeliche Weinachten.

BOY: In Sweden it's God Jul.

GIRL: In Mexico it's Felices Pascuas.

M.C.: But wherever you are, however you say it, it means the same thing: Merry Christmas!

ALL: Merry Christmas! (CHORUS *begins to march around gaily, singing the first two stanzas of "Deck the Halls." As they march they throw sprigs of fir or small red paper bells around the stage. At the end of the second stanza,* M.C. *stops them.*)

M.C.: Wait a minute! Wait a minute! I'm afraid you're starting at the wrong place. "Deck the Halls" shouldn't come at the beginning of the program. You'll be getting everybody all mixed up. (*All* CHORUS *members, except one* GIRL, *go back to their places.*)

GIRL: But it's such a merry song, and we were just talking about a Merry Christmas! (*She does a little jig as she sings.*) "Fa-la-la-la-la, la-la, la-la."

M.C.: Merry, yes, but we have to have some order here, not just a jumble of carols. (*Thumbs through script*) "Deck the Halls" doesn't come until page ten.

GIRL (*Jigging again merrily*): Fa-la-la-la-la, la-la, la-la.

M.C. (*Back at stand, ignoring* GIRL): Ladies and gentlemen, a great deal of obscurity surrounds the origin of many of our favorite Christmas carols, but we are going to do our best to put them in their places. (GIRL *begins to jig again.* M.C. *gently but firmly puts her back in her place in* CHORUS, *then returns to stand.*) In the first place, people have been singing Christmas carols for hundreds and hundreds of years. Let's go back to 1223 A.D., more than seven hundred years ago. It is Christmastide in Assisi, a town in central Italy. The day is cool, but fair, with a gleaming jewel of sun in a clear sky. A peasant approaches, carrying a queer wooden box and a bundle of hay. (PEASANT *enters with box and hay,*

looks around curiously, puts down box and shrugs.)
Something is obviously wrong. He doesn't seem to know
what he is here for. Well, here comes a woodcarver. Perhaps he will know. (1ST WOODCARVER *enters. He carries
wooden figures of animals. He looks around.*)

1ST WOODCARVER: Is this the place?

PEASANT (*Shrugging*): Each man has his own place, so
they say. What place do you mean?

1ST WOODCARVER: I was told to come to the edge of town
near a certain olive tree.

PEASANT: Here's an olive tree, that's certain. What have
you there?

1ST WOODCARVER: An ox, an ass and three sheep, carved of
wood and painted according to instructions.

PEASANT: You, too, had instructions?

1ST WOODCARVER (*Nodding*): From Brother Francis.
(*Looks at* PEASANT'S *box and hay*) But I am afraid I do
not perceive the meaning of *your* instructions. A box of
hay?

PEASANT: Box, indeed! Have you never seen a manger?

1ST WOODCARVER: Oh, a manger. *One* manger for an ox,
an ass, and three sheep? I do not understand.

M.C.: Now, a second woodcarver approaches. He recog-
nizes the first. (2ND WOODCARVER *comes in briskly,
carrying wooden figures.*)

2ND WOODCARVER: Good morrow to you. Where is Brother
Francis?

1ST WOODCARVER: Who can say?

2ND WOODCARVER: I can say I'd like to know the meaning
of all this. Hay. A wooden box. Animals of wood. And
my carved figures.

PEASANT: What figures?

2ND WOODCARVER: A middle-aged man, a young mother,
and a child. At first I hesitated to carve the child. "Such
a child as the Christ Child might have been," Brother

Francis instructed me. How could I carve such a child? How would a stern Judge who fills us with fear and awe look as a child, I wondered. Ah, it was as if Brother Francis read my thoughts.

1ST WOODCARVER: How's that?

2ND WOODCARVER: "Not a Judge!" he told me. "People think of Christ wrongly. I must show them they are mistaken. He is not a dreaded Judge. He is as a friendly, loving child. Can you carve Him so?" (APPRENTICE WOODCARVER, *carrying other figures, enters, and stands listening.*) So I carved a smiling child, like my own son in the cradle! So! (*Holds up figure. Sees* APPRENTICE WOODCARVER.) Who are you?

APPRENTICE WOODCARVER: I am an apprentice woodcarver. My master is ill. He was unable to bring the three kings to the appointed place. (*Puts kings down, takes angels from pocket*) And the angels. (*Somewhat embarrassed*) Brother Francis asked me, a mere apprentice, if I could carve angels. Are they all right?

1ST WOODCARVER (*Appraisingly*): A little small, I should say.

2ND WOODCARVER: On the contrary, not small enough.

PEASANT: Here comes Brother Francis. He will know what is large enough and small enough! (FRANCIS OF ASSISI *enters joyously.*)

FRANCIS: So you are all here, brothers. Ah! I see you have brought what I asked. Now I can teach the people what they must be taught, and in a simple way. I can teach that Christ is not a stern Judge, but a little Child to be loved. (*Bends over box*) The manger is just as I wanted it—not too fine and fancy. (*Puts in some hay*)

PEASANT (*Awed*): The Christ is not to be feared, you say?

FRANCIS: No, no. He is to be loved. Here you see the whole story. (*Gestures at manger and figures*) We shall carry the story into the church and light it with candles, so everyone in Assisi can see.

1ST WOODCARVER: See what, Brother Francis?

FRANCIS (*Laughing*): You do not understand? Then watch me. (*He begins to set up the crèche.*) Here is the manger in Bethlehem, the city of David, where Joseph, who was of the house of David, went to be taxed. Here, brothers, are the humble, friendly beasts in the stable, giving of their warmth that winter night so long ago. (*Places animals around the manger*) This is the little donkey Mary rode from Nazareth, she being great with child. Blessed Mary! (*Places her near the manger*) "And she brought forth her first-born son, and wrapped him in swaddling clothes, and laid him in a manger, because there was no room for them in the inn."

PEASANT: Now I see the need for the manger! And hay for the bed!

FRANCIS: "And there were shepherds in the same district living in the fields and keeping watch over their flock by night." (*To* 1ST WOODCARVER) Your cloak will make an excellent field, brother, being of such a good earthy color. (*Puts cloak to one side, places shepherds on it*) "And behold, an angel of the Lord stood by them . . ."

APPRENTICE (*Holding out angel*): Here is the angel, Brother Francis. Is it too small? Or too large, perhaps?

FRANCIS: Just right, my boy! (*Places angel near shepherds*) "And the glory of the Lord shone round about them."

2ND WOODCARVER: The candles in the church are like the glory of the Lord.

APPRENTICE WOODCARVER (*Intent on the story*): The shepherds were afraid. But the angel told them not to fear, didn't he, Brother Francis?

FRANCIS (*Nodding*): "Behold," he said. "I bring you news of great joy, which shall be to all people. For today in the town of David a Saviour has been born to you, who is Christ the Lord. You shall find Him wrapped in swaddling clothes, lying in a manger."

PEASANT: Aye, a manger.

FRANCIS: "And suddenly, there was with the angel, a multitude of the heavenly host praising God . . ." Come, brothers, we must praise God. We must circle around the manger of God's Son and sing our praises. Christmas is a time of joy, brothers! Christmas is a time for singing. Come, join hands, and sing for the Christ Child in the manger on the holy eve of Christmas. Sing with joy! (*They join hands and circle around the crèche singing "Angels We Have Heard on High."*)

PEASANT, WOODCARVERS, FRANCIS:
"Angels we have heard on high,"
Sweetly singing o'er the plains . . ." (*Etc.*)

CHORUS (*Joining in*): "Gloria . . ." (*Etc.*)

PEASANT, WOODCARVERS, FRANCIS (*Circling the crèche as they sing*):
"Shepherds, why this jubilee," etc.

CHORUS: "Gloria," etc. (PEASANT, WOODCARVERS *and* FRANCIS *begin to move the crèche to back center stage where it will be out of sight behind* CHORUS. CHORUS *parts, standing on both sides temporarily.*)
"Come to Bethlehem and see
Him whose birth the angels sing . . ."
(*Etc.*) (*If the crèche has not been completely moved by the end of the third stanza,* CHORUS *sings fourth stanza, "See Him in a manger laid."* PEASANT, WOODCARVERS *and* FRANCIS *exit behind* CHORUS.)

M.C.: That was the beginning of Christmas caroling, more than seven hundred years ago—the singing for joy around the first crèche of St. Francis of Assisi! That was the beginning. After St. Francis made religion more human by his little drama of the story of the Nativity, special Christmas songs sprang up among the people.

In many places in Italy, peasants and shepherds came down out of the hills at Christmastime, to sing and play their pipes in the villages. Townsfolk who wished to celebrate Christmas would place a wooden spoon outside their door as a signal. (BOY *from* CHORUS *puts out a wooden spoon. In a moment* THREE SHEPHERDS, *rather frightened, come running in.*)

1ST SHEPHERD: What a woman!

2ND SHEPHERD: Her chasing us down the road like that with a stick!

3RD SHEPHERD: Wake her baby, indeed! With our singing? As if her baby wouldn't be lulled to sleep by our singing!

1ST SHEPHERD: Aye. (*Sees spoon*) Look, a spoon. (*Looks back toward wings*) Is it safe? Has she gone? (*Picks up spoon, uses it for baton*) Come, lads, let's give them a song of rejoicing. "O Come, O Come, Emmanuel."

THREE SHEPHERDS:
"O come, O come, Emmanuel,
And ransom captive Israel . . ." (*Etc.*)
(SHEPHERDS *move out at the end of two or three stanzas, taking the spoon with them.*)

M.C.: Rejoice! Rejoice in other countries, too, as well as in Italy. In France, too, songs were being sung to celebrate the Christ Child's birthday. Noël, they called it. Noël for the Christmas birthday! Joyeux Noël! And we still sing one of the shepherd carols of medieval France, "The First Nowell."

BOYS IN CHORUS:
"The first Nowell the angel did say . . ." *Etc.*

CHORUS: "Nowell, Nowell . . ." (*Etc.*)

BOYS IN CHORUS: "Then let us all with one accord . . ." *Etc.*

CHORUS: "Nowell, Nowell . . ." (*Etc.*) (*All five stanzas of "The First Nowell" may be used if desired. During the last chorus, several* CHILDREN *carrying flashlight torches hurry across the stage.*)

M.C.: What was that? Lights? Torches? Yes, of course. We are still in France in the middle ages. We are in Provence, in southeastern France, at Christmas time. There must be a crèche for Christmas Eve in Provence. (CHORUS *parts, so crèche shows.*)

GIRL IN CHORUS (*Calling out*): Torches here, Jeanette, Isabella! Torches here to His cradle run! (JEANETTE *and* ISABELLA, *followed by other* CHILDREN, *come running in again with lights. They stand near the crèche to light it while singing "Bring a Torch, Jeanette, Isabella."*)

GIRL IN CHORUS: "This is Jesus, good folk of the village, Christ is born, 'tis Mary calling."

JEANETTE, ISABELLA *and* CHORUS (*Loudly, crowding to look*):
"Ah! Ah! What a lovely mother!
Ah! Ah! What a lovely Child!"

GIRL IN CHORUS (*Shushing them*):
"Wrong it is, when the Baby is sleeping,
Wrong it is to shout so loud."
(OTHERS, *chagrined, shrink back*)

GIRL IN CHORUS: "Now you there, and you others, be quiet! For at a sound our Jesus wakens."

JEANETTE: Hush!

ISABELLA: Hush!

CHORUS:
"He is sleeping so soundly. Hush! Hush! Hush! Do but see Him sleep!"
(*All look at the crèche. Softly* CHORUS *begins to sing the stanza beginning "Softly now in the narrow stable . . ."* JEANETTE, ISABELLA *and* CHILDREN *who followed them take a final look, then tiptoe out with their torches as* CHORUS *finishes the song. A* GIRL *comes back quietly and stands looking at crèche, her curiosity mixed with*

awe. She begins to sing "What Child Is This?")

GIRL:

"What Child is this, who, laid to rest,
On Mary's lap is sleeping?
Whom angels greet with anthems sweet,
While shepherds watch are keeping?"

CHORUS:

"This, this is Christ the King . . ." (*Etc.*)

GIRL:

"Why lies He in such mean estate,
Where ox and ass are feeding?"

CHORUS: "Good Christian, fear . . ." (*Etc.*)

GIRL (*Speaking*): The Babe, the Son of Mary!

CHORUS: "So bring Him incense, gold and myrrh . . ."
(Etc.) (GIRL *goes out behind* CHORUS *as* CHORUS *closes in front of crèche.*)

M.C.: "Joy, joy, for Christ is born!" Joy—and rejoice—
those are the words for Christmas, over and over again.
Good Christian men, rejoice! That takes us to Germany.
"Good Christian Men, Rejoice" is a German carol of
the Middle Ages. At that time, half of it was written in
German and half in Latin, but for more than four hundred years we have been singing it in English. Rejoice,
good Christian men, at Christmas time!

CHORUS:

"Good Christian men, rejoice
With heart and soul and voice . . ." (*Etc.*)
(*At least two stanzas, more if desired*)

M.C.: Good Christian men in Germany were the first to
rejoice around a Christmas tree, as the Italians were
the first to rejoice around a crèche. It may be just a
legend, but a famous German pastor, Martin Luther, is
credited with bringing home the first Christmas tree. He
also wrote several Christmas songs. (CHORUS *begins to
hum very softly, "Away in a Manger" as background.*)

It is a snowy Christmas Eve in the 1530's. Martin **Luther** is walking home through the woods, thinking of the comfort of home ahead, yet not unmindful of the beauty around him. He sees stars caught in the branches of the fir trees. He thinks of the star that shone down on a stable in Bethlehem on just such a sparkling night many years ago. Why, he thought, can we not bring some of that light into a home on Christmas Eve? Eagerly, he cuts a small fir tree by the roadside and hurries home. (LUTHER *comes in with fir tree.* CHORUS *stops humming.*)

LUTHER: Wife! Wife! My dear Catherine, see here!

CATHERINE (*Stepping from* CHORUS): Sh, Martin. You will wake the children.

LUTHER: Wake the children! Yes, indeed, by all means, I will wake the children, so they may see, too.

CATHERINE: See what?

LUTHER: The glory of Christmas Eve! The light of the star! The light of the Christ Child! (*He sets the tree in a pot or stand.*) Have you some small candles, my dear Catherine, so we can bring the starry heavens right into the house?

CATHERINE: Candles for stars? Why, yes. I made some little candles from the last beeswax.

LUTHER: Let us tie them to the tree! (CATHERINE *starts out for candles.*) And one candle larger than the rest, even as the star of Bethlehem dominated the heavens that night. (*She goes; he admires the tree. She returns with a string of white lights.* LUTHER *and* CATHERINE *put the lights on the tree, with one larger light near the top.*) Under the tree we must arrange the manger scene. Stars above to light the heavens, and Jesus below to light the world!

CATHERINE (*Excited*): How did you ever think of it?

LUTHER: Walking through the woods, meditating on the nativity. (*They finish lights, then arrange the manger scene.* CHORUS *parts so they can arrange it.*) Now call the children, Catherine! (*He continues to work on the crèche while* CATHERINE *goes to get their* SONS *and* DAUGHTER, *who are very sleepy. They are awed by the lighted tree as they enter, and are quickly awake.*)

1ST SON: Where did the shining tree come from?

DAUGHTER: What is it, Father?

2ND SON: It shines like stars in the night.

LUTHER: Do you hear, Catherine? Like stars in the night.

1ST SON (*Looking at manger scene*): I know. You have brought in the stars to shine above the Christ Child's head on his birthday!

DAUGHTER: A birthday tree.

1ST SON: A Christmas tree. (*They join hands and circle around the tree singing "The Christmas Tree."*)

DAUGHTER: Now we must sing your song, father, the one you wrote for us. (*She begins to sing "From Heaven High."*)

"From heaven high I come to you
To bring you tidings strange and true."

SONS (*Joining in*):

"Glad tidings of great joy I bring
Whereof I now will say and sing."

LUTHER *and* CATHERINE (*Joining in*):

"To you this night is born a child
Of Mary, chosen Mother mild . . ." (*Etc.*)

(CHORUS *joins in, marching slowly around stage to give the* LUTHERS *a chance to replace crèche and go out with the Christmas tree.*)

CHORUS:

"Glory to God in highest heaven,
Who unto us His Son hath given!"

(CHORUS *may repeat a stanza to give plenty of time for* LUTHERS *to exit.* CATHERINE *rejoins* CHORUS.)

M.C.: Carols from Italy, carols from England, carols from

France and Germany. (GIRL *steps out from* CHORUS.)

GIRL: What about America? Didn't we make up any carols of our own?

M.C.: Yes, but first we must go back to England.

GIRL: Back to England?

M.C.: We must go back to Elizabethan England, always remembering that England gave us most of our Christmas carols.

GIRL (*Jigging*): "Fa-la-la-la-la, la-la, la-la."

M.C.: As a matter of fact, "Deck the Halls" is an old Welsh carol, full of the spirit of England under the first Queen Elizabeth. In England, as time went on, Christmas became more and more a great festival of merrymaking. The halls of the lords were decked with holly.

CHORUS (*Singing*): "Deck the halls with boughs of holly," (*Etc., to end of first stanza.* GIRL *jigs on the refrain*)

M.C.: Elizabethan England was gay with feasting and singing and games and wassailing at Christmas time. Masked actors called *mummers* presented pantomimes. Roving bands of singers called *waits* went about the streets singing Christmas carols, and hoping to be paid for their efforts. (*A group of* WAITS *come in. They are gaily singing "Wassail Song." They turn toward the audience.*)

WAITS:

"Here we go a-wassailing
Among the leaves of green . . ." (*Etc.*)
(*Turning to* CHORUS, *holding out little leather purses*)
"We have got a little purse
Of stretching leather skin . . ." (*Etc.*)
(WAITS *gather a few coins and replace purses.*)
"Bring us out a table,
And spread it with a cloth . . ." (*Etc.*)
(*They pantomime hungrily.*)
"Good Master and good Mistress

While you sit by the fire . . ." (*Etc.*)

(WAITS *go out, annoyed that they haven't been treated better.*)

M.C.: Christmas in old England! The Yule log—roast goose—plum pudding—singers in the streets—holly and ivy!

GIRL: *Now* do we go to America? To jolly young America?

M.C.: Just a minute! In the early days Christmas was anything but jolly in America.

GIRL: Anything but jolly?

M.C.: The Puritans were opposed to such frivolous sport as singing carols. Early New England colonists even forbade the celebration of Christmas. In 1644, the Puritans declared December 25th to be a market day instead of a holiday, and forbade anyone to have plum pudding or mince pie. Later, they even fined anyone who stopped work or feasted on Christmas Day.

GIRL: So we didn't have any carols in the early days? Or any holiday? Or any mince pie?

M.C.: That's right. But strangely enough, about that very time, the first American carol was born. Not in New England. In New France. The time is around 1640. Father Jean de Brebeuf, Jesuit missionary to the Huron Indians on the neck of land between Lake Huron, Lake Erie, and Lake Ontario, is rehearsing a group of Indians for the celebration of Christmas just a few days off. He has composed a carol for them in their own language. But he has no organ. The Indians have only tom-toms and rattles. So Father Brebeuf used words that would fit a tom-tom accompaniment. Here is the English translation. (*Several members of the* CHORUS *begin to beat muted drums to the rhythm of "God Rest You Merry, Gentlemen." A* BOY *who has slipped on an Indian head-dress steps from* CHORUS *to chant words of the carol.*)

BOY:

" 'Twas in the moon of wintertime,
When all the birds had fled,
That mighty Gitchi Manitou
Sent angel choirs instead.
Before their light the stars grew dim,
And hunters heard the hymn:"

CHORUS (*Joining chant*):

"Jesus, your King, is born;
Jesus is born,
In Excelsis Gloria!" (*Several* INDIAN BRAVES *with bows
and arrows come in from wings. They kneel in rever-
ence.*)

1ST INDIAN BRAVE:

"In the lodge of broken bark
The tender babe was found;
A ragged robe of rabbit skin
Enwrapped his beauty round.
And as the hunter braves drew nigh,
The angel song rang high:"

CHORUS (*Joining chant*):

"Jesus, your King, is born;
Jesus is born,
In Excelsis Gloria!" (*3* INDIAN CHIEFS *come in from
wings. They carry pelts, and kneel and offer their gifts.*)

2ND INDIAN BRAVE:

"Earliest moon of winter time
Is not so round and fair
As was the ring of glory
On the helpless infant there,
While chiefs from far before him knelt
With gifts of beaver pelt."

CHORUS: "Jesus, your King, is born . . ." (*Etc.*)

3RD INDIAN BRAVE:

"The children of the forest free,
O sons of Manitou,

The Holy Child of earth and heaven
Is born today for you.
Come kneel before the radiant boy
Who brings you peace and joy:"

CHORUS:

"Jesus, your King, is born;
Jesus is born,
In Excelsis Gloria!" (CHORUS *repeats chorus as* INDIANS *exit.*)

M.C.: The first American Christmas carol! Few of us have ever heard it sung. The Christ Child in a bark lodge instead of in a manger! Wrapped in a rabbit skin instead of swaddling clothes! Wandering hunters instead of shepherds hearing the angel choir! Indian chiefs coming from afar with their gifts of fox and beaver skins, instead of three Wise Men with gold, frankincense and myrrh! Christmas in the New World!

As America was settled, of course, the Puritans were outvoted. Carols from the "old country" came over with the settlers, and Christmas became a joyous occasion up and down the Atlantic seaboard.

Meanwhile, the English produced another famous Christmas carol. It was written by the great English hymn writer of the eighteenth century, Isaac Watts. He was working on a book, telling the psalms of David in his own words, when his inspiration came. He was reading the 98th Psalm. (ISAAC WATTS *enters with Bible, reads aloud.*)

WATTS: "Make a joyful noise unto the Lord, all the earth: make a loud noise, and rejoice, and sing praise. Sing unto the Lord with the harp; with the harp, and the voice of a psalm. For he cometh to judge the earth; with righteousness shall he judge the world, and the people with equity." (*Looks up*) Make a joyful noise, for he cometh! What a test for a song! A Christmas song of joy. (*Hums*) Joy to the world! The Lord is come—

CHORUS (*Taking up carol, "Joy to the World"*):
"Let earth receive her King. . . ." (*Etc.*)

WATTS (*Singing second stanza as solo*):
"Joy to the world!
The Saviour reigns . . ." (*Etc.*)

CHORUS (*Singing third stanza as* WATTS *goes out*): "He rules
the world with truth and grace . . ." (*Etc.*)

M.C.: Carols from Italy, carols from France, carols from
England and Germany! But we have to go to Austria
for one of the most beloved carols of all. (GIRL *steps
out from* CHORUS *and starts to jig.*)

GIRL: To Austria we go! Fa-la-la-la-la, la-la, la-la. (*Others
pull her back.*)

M.C.: We go to the little town of Obendorf in the Austrian
Alps. It is a sparkling cold night, just before Christmas,
1818. The mountains are covered with snow, the air is
clear, almost brittle, the sky bright with stars. Joseph
Mohr, 26-year-old vicar of the little church, is hurrying
down the village street to call on his friend Franz Gruber, the schoolmaster, who plays the organ at church.
Father Mohr has a piece of paper in his pocket to show
the schoolmaster-organist. Now he is at his friend's
door. Now he is ushered into the house, to warm himself
at the stove. (FATHER MOHR *and* FRANZ GRUBER *enter.*)

GRUBER: A cold night to be abroad, Father.

MOHR: But calm and bright. I was struck by the brightness when I returned to my room after meeting with the
children of the parish. (*Smiles*) The same children you
know and teach, my dear Franz.

GRUBER: Ach, and their minds full of nothing but Christmas!

MOHR: I am afraid that is the state of my mind, too. Soon
We shall be celebrating the Nativity. My thoughts were
full of it as I walked home. I wished for some new way

to celebrate, something a little different for the boys to sing in church on Christmas eve. (*He takes the paper from his pocket, thrusts it at* GRUBER.) Here, tell me what you think, Franz, as a schoolmaster and organist, not as a friend who might be prejudiced.

GRUBER (*Reading aloud*):
"Silent night! Holy night!
All is calm, all is bright . . ."
(*He reads in silence for a moment, then looks up excitedly.*) Why, it is beautiful, Father. Where did it come from?

MOHR: I—well, I wrote it. Do you think the words could make a song, Franz?

GRUBER: Yes, yes. Indeed, yes. (*Looks at words, beats time to imaginary tune.*)

MOHR (*Urgently*): Can you do it, Franz? You can play the organ, you have instruction in music. Can you set it to music right away, for the Christmas celebration? I know there is little time, but will you try?

GRUBER: I will try. (*Looks at words again, becomes absorbed.* FATHER MOHR *smiles and tiptoes out.*)

M.C.: Franz Gruber, the 29-year-old schoolmaster, wrote music for the vicar's words, but when he went to try the song on the organ, the organ refused to play. It was old and there were mice in it! Still, Father Mohr must have his new song for the Christmas festivities. So the schoolmaster taught the children to sing the song with only a guitar for accompaniment. (GRUBER *turns to* CHORUS *and directs the singing of "Silent Night," either* a capella *or with only a guitar accompaniment.*)

SOLO BOY:
"Silent night, holy night,
All is calm, all is bright
Round yon Virgin Mother and Child,"

CHORUS (*Softly*):

"Holy Infant so tender and mild,
Sleep in heavenly peace,
Sleep in heavenly peace."

(*Second and third stanzas also should be sung with solo parts and* CHORUS. *During the last chorus,* GRUBER *exits.*)

M.C.: Gradually, Father Mohr's wonderful song spread through Austria and Germany. It became popular wherever it was heard. In 1833, twenty-five years after it was written, "Silent Night" was sung at a Christmas concert in Leipzig. From that time its fame was assured. Now it belongs to the world!

Carols have come from Christians of all nationalities and races—from the Czechs, the Chinese, the Croatians; from the Scandinavians, the Sicilians, the Poles; from the Puerto Ricans, the Russians, and even from Negro slaves in the United States before the Civil War. Here is one of the carols the slaves gave us:

BOY (*Swinging into "Rise Up, Shepherd, and Follow"*): "There's a star in the East on Christmas morn,"

CHORUS: "Rise up, shepherd, and follow." (*Throughout the spiritual,* CHORUS *comes in only on "Rise up, shepherd, and follow."* BOY *carries the other lines.*)

M.C.: And now here is a strange coincidence. In Austria, Father Mohr and his church organist produced "Silent Night" as something different for the children of the parish to sing for Christmas. Fifty years later, an Episcopalian rector in Philadelphia and his organist composed a new carol for the children of *their* Sunday School to sing as something different. The song was as speedily written and as speedily set to music as was "Silent Night." It, too, became world famous. The American rector's name was Phillips Brooks; his organist was Lewis Redner. (BROOKS *and* REDNER *enter.*)

REDNER: A cold night to be abroad, isn't it, sir?

BROOKS: But calm and bright, Redner. As I walked home

from the meeting at the church, I was struck by the brightness. On just such a night three years ago, I was in the Holy Land. I will never forget it. I was riding horseback from Jerusalem to Bethlehem, following the stars.

REDNER: How does Bethlehem look by starlight? I've often wondered.

BROOKS: It's on a hill, you know. Just five miles from Jerusalem. By day it isn't much of a town, but at night— (*Takes paper from pocket*) Redner, you know I have been wishing for some new way to celebrate Christmas this year, something a little different for the children to sing. (*Holds out paper*) Here, tell me what you think of this. Do you see anything in it?

REDNER (*Taking paper, reading aloud*):
"O little town of Bethlehem,
How still we see thee lie!
Above thy deep and dreamless sleep
The silent stars go by;
Yet in thy dark streets shineth
The everlasting Light . . ." (*Looks up*) Where did you find it?

BROOKS: I wrote it. Perhaps I should say it wrote itself, out of my memories. Do you think it would make a song?

REDNER: I should say it would! (*Studies words, drumming rhythm*)

BROOKS: Will you do it, Redner? Will you set it to music right away? I know there isn't much time. This is Saturday evening. Tomorrow is the last day of Sunday School before Christmas.

REDNER: I will try. A tune is opening up already. (*He is engrossed with the paper.* BROOKS *smiles and tiptoes out.*)

M.C.: Sure enough, the church organist had his rector's words set to music in time for Sunday School the next morning, and the song has been heard at Chirstmas time ever since. (REDNER *directs* CHORUS *in "O Little Town of Bethlehem," all four stanzas if desired. At the end of the song, he joins* CHORUS.) Hundreds of Christmas songs and carols have been writen over the centuries. We couldn't begin to sing them all on one program, but we still have time for one of the oldest and most famous of all Christmas songs. The tune is attributed to St. Bonaventura, who lived in the thirteenth century. The song has been translated into more than a hundred languages and dialects, and every year it is sung in Christian churches throughout the world. "Adeste Fideles—O Come All Ye Faithful."

CHORUS:

"O come, all ye faithful, joyful and triumphant . . ." (*Etc.*) (M. C. *gestures for audience to join in.* CHORUS *and audience sing at least two stanzas.*)

THE END

Sing the Songs of Lincoln

Characters

READER
NANCY HANKS LINCOLN
SARAH LINCOLN (SAIRY)
ABRAHAM LINCOLN (ABE)
THOMAS LINCOLN (TOM)
DENNIS HANKS
ELIZABETH JOHNSTON
JOHNNY JOHNSTON
SQUARE DANCERS
FIDDLER
SARAH BUSH JOHNSTON LINCOLN
ANN RUTLEDGE
TWO MEN
BAND AND CAMPAIGNERS
YOUNG WOMAN
WOMAN FROM VIRGINIA
GIRL
JOHN HAY
ACTORS
OFFSTAGE CHORUS

BEFORE RISE: READER *enters in front of curtain, takes place at reading stand at one side, and opens book.*

---

* Most of the songs in this play can be found in *Songs that Lincoln Loved* by John Lair, Duell, Sloan and Pearce, N. Y., and Little, Brown and Company, Boston, 1954.

READER: She had something of a singing voice, Nancy Hanks Lincoln had. But she didn't have much to sing about . . . leastwise most women wouldn't think so. Most women nowadays wouldn't be in a singing mood with a life like hers. Maybe, in a way, that's why Nancy Lincoln sang, to forget the drudgery and the hardships and the poverty . . . the washing and cooking and scrubbing, the spinning and weaving and soapmaking, the sewing and patching and fixing . . . (*The curtain rises.*)

SETTING: *A one-room cabin, furnished in frontier fashion.*

AT RISE: NANCY HANKS LINCOLN *comes in with old clothes to patch over her arm. She sits on a stool, humming tune of "William Riley"* * *as she sews.*

READER: No, Nancy Hanks didn't have much to sing about after she'd been married to Tom Lincoln for ten years. Not that he was a mean man . . . not that he was any worse a provider than other farmers in the cabin country of Kentucky. Still, he wasn't what you'd call enterprising, and as a rolling stone he had an uncanny way of choosing the wrong direction to roll. (NANCY, *taking her sewing with her, goes to cabin door and looks out, peering up the road and calling hopefully.*)

NANCY: Sairy! Abe! (*When she receives no answer, she goes back to her sewing.*)

READER: The first two years in Elizabethtown, Kentucky, weren't so bad, when Tom Lincoln was carpentering. That's where Sarah, their first baby, was born. The next three years on the South Fork of Nolin's Creek where Tom was trying to farm were harder. That's where Abe was born, in a small log cabin with a dirt floor and only one window, and a stick-and-clay fireplace. (NANCY, *restless, goes to door again.*)

NANCY: Abe! Sairy! (*After a moment, she turns, puts wood on fire.*)

READER: When Abe was two years old, Tom Lincoln moved his family again, to a farm on Knob Creek, close to the old Cumberland Trail. That's where another son was born—named after his father. But little Thomas died when he was three days old, and Nancy Lincoln didn't sing again for a while. (NANCY *pulls her old shawl around her, looks off dreamily, then resumes her work.*) Things didn't improve any at Knob Creek. But when Nancy's voice came back, she sang in spite of everything because Abe and Sarah urged her on. They liked to sit and listen, learning the tunes and words. (NANCY *sings a stanza or two of "William Riley."* NOTE: *An offstage chorus, or offstage soloists, may be substituted for onstage singing throughout the play.*) Then when Sarah was nine and Abe seven, Tom Lincoln's title to the Knob Creek farm came under question. Silent and discouraged, he went off, heading north, across the Ohio River to Indiana where government land was up for sale at two dollars an acre. Surely nobody could question a government title. (NANCY *gets up to put something in the iron kettle at the fireplace. She looks out expectantly when she passes the door, then goes back to her patching.*) At the Knob Creek farm Nancy Lincoln waited for Tom to return, wondering what the future held. She burdened herself with work so that the children could go to school. And she felt singing glad to do it! (NANCY *sings the first two stanzas of "Barbara Allen."*)

SAIRY (*Coming in with a rather heavy buckskin bag*): Here's the meal, Mammy. Abe's got the rest of it. (*Goes to fire to warm hands*) The sun doesn't make any heat today, seems like.

NANCY: That's the way with a December sun, Sairy.

Where's Abe?

SAIRY: Talking to the miller's wife. I warned him I wouldn't wait for him. I reckon he won't get lost, though.

NANCY: I reckon not. (*Then apologetically*) It grieved me to have you and Abe lose part of a day at school to tote that corn to the mill, Sairy. Goodness knows you don't get to school half enough as it is. But we were clean out of meal. I wish your Pappy'd come back . . .

SAIRY: Is Indianny far, Mammy?

NANCY: A good piece.

SAIRY: Is the land really better there?

NANCY: That's what your Pappy heard. Wanted to go see for himself. Couldn't be much worse'n this creek bottom where the crops wash out, come a bad rain.

SAIRY: I hope we don't have to move to Indianny, though. Here it's only two miles to school, and maybe there won't be any school at all over there. The teacher says Abe's got a learning mind.

NANCY (*Nodding*): A learning mind and a dreaming one. But there's nothing to do if your Pappy gets it in his head to move.

ABE (*Bursting in with bag of meal*) : Mammy, the miller's wife calls it "Barbara *Ellen*" 'stead of *Allen,* and her words are all different.

NANCY: Barbara Ellen, Barbara Allen—reckon there's a dozen ways to sing it. I sing the way I remember it from my mammy; the miller's wife sings what she remembers from hers. When it's not written down, and when we couldn't read it if it were, who's to say what's right? That's why I want you to get all the learning you can, Abe. It's the only way to be sure.

SAIRY: Your song's best, Mammy. (*She starts to sing the song, and the others join in. The singing is suddenly interrupted by the appearance of* TOM LINCOLN.)

TOM (*At the door*): Gets so a man can't hear himself think in his own house.

NANCY (*With surprise, hurrying to door*): Tom! You're back!

SAIRY *and* ABE (*Standing back*) : Pappy!

TOM: Rustle up some wood, Abe. Get a kettle on to boil, Sairy. I shot us a wild turkey, coming through the woods. Hoecakes taste mighty good with fresh game, Nancy. (*They scatter to their tasks.* TOM *throws off his pack and coat.*) Reckon we can be ready to start in a few days?

NANCY: Where to, Tom?

TOM: Indianny. No use waiting for the weather to get *colder*. I'd like to be over there and settled before year-end, and it's a good piece away. (*Glances at* ABE, *who slips out for the wood.*)

NANCY (*Grasping at hope*): Settled? There's a cabin then, or somewhere to stay?

TOM (*With a grunt*): Cabin! We'll be lucky if we get ourselves a pole-shed before the snow piles up. It's wild, unbroken country, Nancy, but there'll be deep rich soil once we get a clearing. I've never seen such big oaks and elms, and sycamores and maples and birches, looped up and around with wild grapevines. Never seen such cover for game. We won't be going hungry for meat this winter, I can tell you that.

SAIRY (*Tentatively*): And Indians . . . ?

TOM: Caught sight of nary an Indian all the time in Indianny.

NANCY: Any folks to neighbor with, Tom?

TOM: Not enough to cause any bother. One family every square mile, I reckon.

ABE (*Coming in with wood in time to hear*): Any school?

TOM: Not closer'n eight-nine miles. But you young 'uns won't have time for schooling anyhow, what with all the work to be done. Have to carry spring water almost a mile for one thing. That's a job for you and Sairy, Abe. (*Turns toward door*) Well, I'll be walking over to Redman's to see about selling the cows and chickens and extry corn. Best start packing, Nancy.

SAIRY: How far is it, Pappy?

TOM: Reckon a hundred miles, the way we'll have to go. Only about fifty, could we fly like crows . . . which we can't. (*Goes out*)

NANCY (*Looking after him*): Sometimes when you don't feel much like it, it's the best time for singing.

ABE: The "Ninety-Fifth," Mammy?

NANCY: "Bound for Canaan" would be better, Abe. And maybe it *will* be a land o' promise over there in Indianny. Can't ever tell. (*They are singing "Bound for Canaan" as the curtain falls.*)

READER: Turned out Indiana wasn't a land of promise for Nancy Hanks Lincoln and her family. They reached Tom's wilderness claim near Pigeon Creek with not much more than the clothes on their backs. Wind whistled through the bare treetops and frost shone white on the leaf mold, and streaks of feeble sunlight patterned the ground between close-growing trees.

Tom Lincoln set about building what settlers called a half-faced camp—three sides of logs and boughs and the fourth side open—and that's where the Lincolns spent the winter, hovering around the fire they kept burning at the open side. When Tom was off in the woods, Nancy sang to the children to keep up their spirits. (NANCY *sings snatches of "Barbara Allen" from offstage.*) In the spring, when Abe was eight, he helped his father clear a small piece of ground to plant corn and wheat. With the help of neighbors they built a log cabin with a dirt floor and no windows. Finally, along toward the end of summer, they got around to chinking it and daubing the cracks with mud. They turned the half-faced camp over to Nancy's aunt and uncle who'd come to find the promised land, too. They brought along their adopted son, Dennis Hanks, almost ten years older than Abe. (DENNIS, *about 18, and* ABE, *8, come in before curtain.*)

DENNIS: You catch onto the words quick enough, Abe, but what you do to the tune I can't figure.

ABE: The tune sounds all right inside my head. It just comes out different somehow, Dennis.

DENNIS: Try it again now. Listen hard how the tune goes. (DENNIS *sings the first stanza of "None Can Love Like an Irishman."*)

"The turban'd Turk, who scorns the world,

May strut about with his whiskers curled . . ." (*He accents the beats heavily.*) All right, give me the first two lines.

ABE (*Trying to sing*): "The turban'd Turk . . ." (*Etc.*)

DENNIS: Let your voice out full, like me. Start over. (ABE *and* DENNIS *sing the first two lines with anything but harmony.* DENNIS *is baffled.*) What are you singing a different song for, Abe?

ABE: I wasn't singing a different song. (*Begins to laugh*) I was singing the turban'd Turk all the time. (*They both laugh.*)

DENNIS: Guess what you need is a harmonica. You could carry a tune on that without having to sing it. Yep, that's what you need.

ABE: Papp'd never buy me one, and I've got nothing to trade.

DENNIS: Maybe you can trade work some time, chopping wood or something. I've never seen a young 'un handle an axe the way you can, Abe. If you could sing the way you chop, you'd be the champion singer in the state of Indianny. (*They go out.*)

READER: Nancy Lincoln lived in the new cabin less than

a year. Come the fall of 1818, an epidemic swept through southern Indiana. Nancy's aunt and uncle in the half-faced camp caught the fever and died. Then on October 5, when leaves were fluttering bright in the treetops and a purple haze showed beyond the knoll, Nancy herself took sick. Tom Lincoln did what he could to make her comfortable, but there was little enough to do. Abe and Sarah stood by, frightened and silent.

Their mother never sang again . . . and for a long time Abe could find no music inside of him. (*Offstage chorus sings "Ninety-Fifth."*) The year after Nancy Lincoln's death was a year young Abe would never forget. Twelve-year-old Sarah did her best to keep the cabin orderly, the stew kettle boiling, the clothes patched. Ten-year-old Abe chopped wood and helped tend the crops, but his mind whirled with questions. Why did his mother, his good, kind mother, have to die? Why was his father so dark and silent? What was going to happen to them off in the wilderness? Even the humor of Dennis Hanks failed to rout Abe's melancholy.

Then in November, Tom Lincoln went back to Elizabethtown, Kentucky, to find himself another wife. (*Curtain opens on yard in front of Lincoln cabin. There is a chopping block and wood. Front of cabin shows.* ABE *sits on a log deep in thought.* DENNIS, *now 20, comes in singing lustily a stanza of "None Can Love Like an Irishman." He stops in front of* ABE.)

DENNIS: What you doing, Abe?

ABE: Thinking.

DENNIS: What about?

ABE: About Pappy bringing someone to take Mammy's place. Can't he see there can't be anyone to take her place?

DENNIS: Maybe it won't be so bad.

ABE: Or so good. *You* know how Mammy was, Dennis. She

was your kin. Couldn't anyone be better. (SAIRY *comes out of cabin, a shawl around her shoulders.*)

SAIRY: You'd best bring in a pile o' wood. If they come today, they'll be wanting a good fire, to thaw out.

DENNIS: Nice bright December day like this? (*He sits next to* ABE.)

SAIRY: It's not warm, though. (*She shivers.*) Leastwise I'm cold. (*She shivers again.*) Reckon maybe I'm just plain skeered . . . (ABE *looks at her quickly, somewhat surprised.*)

ABE: What you skeered of, Sairy?

SAIRY: If Pappy's new wife can't find a liking for me, or me for her . . . (*She sighs.*) You can be outdoors, you and Dennis. A girl's got to be indoors most of the time, helping.

DENNIS: Looks as if we're all skeered. (*Rises*) Reckon Sairy's right about the wood, Abe.

ABE: We've been getting ready for them every afternoon for a week, and no sign of 'em yet.

DENNIS: They're bound to get here *some* time. (*He carries an armload of wood into cabin, returning with his gun.* ABE *and* SAIRY *sit side by side on the log.*) You finish the wood, Abe. I reckon after that long drive from Kentucky they might fancy a little fresh game for supper. (*Starts off*) Now don't you go working too hard, you two!

ABE (*Glumly*): Can't anyone take her place.

SAIRY (*Trying to be comforting*): But Mammy wouldn't want us to be sad, Abe. She never had things easy, but she wasn't sad.

ABE: Not that she let us see.

SAIRY: I still remember all the songs. When you and Dennis are away, I sing them to keep myself company. Do you remember them, Abe?

ABE (*Nodding*): But Dennis thinks I sing like a donkey, and I reckon I do.

SAIRY: When I'm a-working around and singing, I don't have so much time to be skeered.

ABE: Doing things helps. (*Gets up, picks up armload of wood and takes it into cabin. On the way back he pauses at the door, listening, cocking his head.*) Hear anything, Sairy?

SAIRY: A little wind in the last oak leaves.

ABE: Something like music . . . way off.

SAIRY (*Listening intently*): Seems like I *do* hear something. Can't be wagon wheels, can it, Abe?

ABE: Maybe. But something else, too, above the sound of wheels grinding and creaking. (*Listens again*) Listen! It's "Bound for Canaan." There's someone a-coming singing "Bound for Canaan."

SAIRY: Do you think it's *her*—Pappy's new wife?

ABE: It's more than just her . . . (*Sound of singing comes faintly from offstage, getting louder gradually.*) Look! There's Pappy with a big old wagon and hosses.

SAIRY: *She's* a-sitting on the seat next to him. And look at all the stuff, Abe! A real true bureau, and a table, and chairs, and feather beds! And three children . . . perched on the load. Singing for all get-out. Two girls and a boy.

ABE: 'Pears to me only two of them's singing. The biggest girl's playing a harmonica, Sairy. A harmonica!

SAIRY: I'm not skeered so much now. When they come a-singing, it's a good sign, don't you think? Mammy'd run out to meet them with her arms open, I know she would. (SAIRY *runs excitedly toward the wings, arms outstretched.* ABE *stands watching doubtfully as the curtain falls.*)

READER: They came a-singing . . . Sarah Bush Lincoln and her three young 'uns. And before the month was out Abe was beginning to sing, too, not so Dennis Hanks could hear, but down inside where it mattered most.

First off the new stepmother stretched out her arms to Abe, and laughed good-naturedly when he drew back. She could wait.

Solemnly Abe watched the unloading. His new mammy had brought something besides furniture and feather beds and shiny pots and pans. She'd brought books, a few wonderful books! And then there was the harmonica her oldest daughter Elizabeth could play. (ABE *and* ELIZABETH *come before curtain.*)

ABE: Where'd you get it, Betsy?

ELIZABETH: It belonged to my Pappy, Mr. Johnston. When he died . . . well, he didn't need it any more. He could play real good.

ABE: So can you. I heard you a long way off.

ELIZABETH: Only "Bound for Canaan" and "Ninety-Fifth." That's all I've practiced. It's harder'n singing.

ABE: Not for *me* it wouldn't be. I'm no shakes when it comes to singing. Ask my cousin Dennis.

ELIZABETH: Well, I'm no shakes playing the harmonica.

ABE: You know "Barbara Allen"? That was my mother's favorite song.

ELIZABETH: I know it to sing, sort of. (*Tries to play it*) It doesn't go right on the harmonica, though. (*Tries again*) *You* try, Abe.

ABE: Me? What do I do?

ELIZABETH: Just pull back and forth with your breath. (*She wipes the harmonica on her apron and hands it to* ABE. *He tries tentatively.*) That's right, in and out. (ABE *gets the first few notes of "Barbara Allen."*) That's *good.* (*He gets a few more notes.*) Real good. I can almost tell what you're playin'. You can practice the rest of the day if you want.

ABE: Honest? I'll do something for you, Betsy . . . whittle you something, make you a buckskin pouch . . .

ELIZABETH: Maybe you can tell me a story . . . all for my-self.

ABE: Wait till Dennis hears me keep in tune tonight! (*They hurry out.*)

READER: He had music in his bones, Abe did, if not in his voice. He had rhythm. When he was twelve years old, he began making up poems and songs. Not that he ever talked much about it. Folks thought of him as a mimic and a storyteller, not a poet. But he had one good audience—his stepmother. She fancied Abe was one of the best rhymesters she ever listened to. Fact is, most everything Abe did struck his stepmother as right smart. She urged Abe to go to school every chance he got, and stood up for him whenever his father talked against too much "eddication."

Oh, life was good for Abe and Sairy and Dennis Hanks after Sarah Bush Lincoln came to live in the log cabin. Her son, Johnny, a year or two younger than Abe, followed him around like a pet dog.

Abe grew lanky and rawboned and muscular. In the woods, wielding an axe, he moved with skill and sureness. He didn't look awkward even with his arms too long for his shirt sleeves and his legs too long for his jeans. But in the presence of young ladies he felt shy and ill-at-ease and ungainly . . . until the sound of music won him over. (ABE *and* JOHNNY JOHNSTON *enter before curtain.* ABE *is 16,* JOHNNY *14.*)

JOHNNY: We can stand here and look in Gentry's window, Abe, if you're skeered to go in. But it's kind of cold out here just lookin'. Betsy and Tilda's inside, and so's Sairy. And you know 'most everybody else. No reason to be skeered. If I were old as you, know what I'd do?

ABE: You'd be right in there at the play-party, Johnny, singing at the top of your voice. (DENNIS HANKS, *26, enters in time to hear.*)

DENNIS: Better not go urgin' Abe to sing at the top of *his* voice, Johnny. (*To* ABE) Come on in, Abe. You know how the dances go from just watchin'. Nobody's going to hurt a big feller like you. Listen . . . they're a-startin' "Old Sister Phoebe." (ABE, JOHNNY, *and* DENNIS *move to one side as curtain opens on a square dance group. A fiddler is playing the tune of "Old Sister Phoebe;" others are dancing.* [NOTE: *See page 23 of "Songs Lincoln Loved" for dance instructions and music.*] *After several stanzas,* ABE *takes out his harmonica and follows the tune. His sister* SARAH *calls out. Music down.*)

SAIRY: That sounds like Abe out there. Come on in, Abe!

ELIZABETH: Johnny's there, too, if Abe is.

SAIRY: And Dennis, your chief partner, Betsy.

OTHERS (*Calling*): Come on in, you-all. We're going to have "Skip to My Lou." (FIDDLER *takes up tune of "Skip to My Lou."* ABE *and others join group, with* SAIRY *taking* ABE *as partner. After a number of stanzas the curtain falls.*)

READER: When Abe was 17, he stood six feet four inches tall. That was the year his sister Sarah and Aaron Grigsby were married. Abe wanted to do something different and special to celebrate the occasion, so he decided to work up a song. (ABE *and* DENNIS *enter before curtain.* DENNIS *is reading something written on rough paper.*)

DENNIS: Not bad a'tall, Abe. Who's a-goin' to sing it?

ABE (*Laughing*): Figured they might stand my voice if I half-chanted like.

DENNIS: Let's hear how you aim to do it. (ABE *half-chants first stanza of "Adam and Eve's Wedding Song."*) Reckon they can understand the words all right. 'Tain't everyone has a song special for their wedding.

ABE: 'Taint everyone has a sister like Sairy, either. (*Looks off dreamily*) Sometimes I get a feeling about it, Dennis . . . I know she loves Aaron, and he'll be good to her

. . . but I wish she weren't getting married and all. I have a foreboding.

DENNIS: Girls can't stay home forever, Abe. She'll be happy with Aaron. Come on, let's hear more of the song. (*Looks at paper*) "The Lord took a bone from Adam and made a woman." Then what? (ABE *sings third and fourth stanzas.* DENNIS *repeats last line of last stanza*) "So she must be protected from injuries and harm." That ought to take care of your foreboding, Abe.

ABE: Anything happen to Sairy, I'd feel mighty bad. (*They go out.*)

READER: Poor Abe. The next year Sairy died and the sorrow of it bit to the marrow of Abe's bones. He felt numbed and melancholy again, the way he did when his mother died. His heart lost its singing. Oh, he was old enough to know that time heals wounds, that melancholy passes, that sooner or later life swings back to normal. But the interlude was hard. He jumped at a chance to help Allen Gentry build a flatboat and load it with farm produce to take down to New Orleans, thinking it would help him forget.

He was gone three months, seeing things, hearing things, smelling things he never knew existed. And thinking things. Abe grew mightily in those three months, in more ways than one. He saw slavery in practice . . . men and women sold at auction in New Orleans . . . just because they had the wrong color skin. He saw slaves working and singing in the fields, singing around campfires at night, even singing when their backs were bent with burdens. (*If desired, an offstage chorus may sing "Now Let Me Fly Away," or "Steal Away," etc., which can be found in "The Fireside Book of Folk Songs," Simon and Schuster, 1947.*)

Back home again, Abe was caught up in the excitement of the election of 1828. Now that he was 19 and had seen a big piece of his country from a flatboat, now that he had watched the waterfront, and walked the streets of New Orleans, and visited the slave market, and listened to all kinds of talk, he felt equal to entering into election talk. John Quincy Adams was running for a second term against Andrew Jackson, a man of the frontier. Adams stood for the rich, Jackson for men who knew hardship and work. (*Curtain opens on the Lincoln cabin.* SARAH BUSH LINCOLN *is knitting,* ABE *is sitting on a stool, writing.*)

ABE: Reckon Jackson's going to get elected come November, Mammy?

SARAH: Why, I've not bothered my head much about it, Abe. Always did say politics is for the menfolks.

ABE: Jackson's a man of the people, people like us. Nothing fancy and high-stepping about him.

SARAH: If he's a man of the people, I reckon they'll elect him. I notice most people have common sense even if they haven't much education. You writing a campaign speech, Abe?

ABE: Only four lines so far, as they came to my mind. You recollect the tune of "Auld Lang Syne," Mammy?

SARAH: 'Course I do. (*Stops her work to hum the tune and beat time*)

ABE: Let's see how this goes, then, with you taking the tune and me saying the words. All right, from the beginning . . .

Let auld acquaintance be forgot
And never brought to mind;
May Jackson be our President,
And Adams left behind.

SARAH: Why, Abe! That's real good, good enough to be put in a book. Reckon you won't ever get a chance to be President, but I'm countin' on you turning into a powerful big poet or something. (*Curtain*)

READER: Abe had just turned 21, just come of age, when Tom Lincoln sold the Pigeon Creek farm. A week later the Lincolns, with Dennis Hanks and his family, packed up their belongings and turned their ox teams toward central Illinois. To Tom Lincoln, always hankering after a land of milk and honey, Illinois sounded like the promised land. Didn't the very name of the river there —Sangamo—mean "the land of plenty" to the Indians? (*Offstage chorus swings into "Bound for Canaan."*) Abe had come of age . . . but it took him a few years to find himself. He tried splitting rails for wages and keep; he took another cargo down to New Orleans; he read books and studied grammar, and clerked in a store; he enlisted in the militia in the Black Hawk War; he went into the store business with a partner and lost money; he became postmaster of the frontier town of New Salem, Illinois; he ran survey lines; he studied law, and tried his luck at politics. When he was 25 years old, he ran for the State Legislature and was elected. And then he fell in love with Ann Rutledge. (*Curtain up on dimly-lit stage, an outdoor scene in spring.* ABE *and* ANN *enter.*)

ABE (*Looking around*): It was here I first heard you sing, Miss Ann. I was walking by myself in the evening, watching the shadows creep over the woods, when I heard your voice. I stood still to listen . . . and I stood still for a long time after the song was finished.

ANN: And how did you know who was singing, Mr. Lincoln?

ABE: Hadn't I been boarding at your father's tavern for a good long time? Hadn't I watched you more than once from my place at the table? And I knew from talk around that the tavern-keeper's daughter had a singing voice. It didn't take a lawyer to put two and two together.

ANN: But you *are* a lawyer, Mr. Lincoln.

ABE: Not yet. Though I'm resolutely determined to become one. Next year perhaps I can get my license.

ANN: Well then, you're *almost* a lawyer, and a Congressman in the Legislature, too. And you're still so young.

ABE: Makes me feel old as the hills sometimes to recollect I was 26 on the twelfth of February last.

ANN (*With a sigh*): Sometimes I feel old as the hills, too.

ABE: I know. I know what you've been through with John McNamar . . . the uncertainty and all, and him off in the East someplace. Have you heard from him lately?

ANN: No. I haven't had a letter for months. I wrote him asking him to release me from our engagement, and he hasn't bothered to answer.

ABE (*Eagerly*): If he hasn't answered, you can consider yourself free, can't you, Miss Ann?

ANN: I consider myself so. Yes, now I do. But oh, for months I've been so forlorn and weary. (*Sings softly from "Pilgrim Stranger"*)

"Here in this country, so dark and dreary,
I long have wander'd, forlorn and weary . . ."

ABE: That's the song you were singing the night I heard you! A song about a pilgrim and a stranger. Those are the words that came to me in the shadows. It would pleasure me more than I can say to hear you sing them again.

ANN: And it would pleasure me to sing them. (ANN *sings first, second, and fourth stanzas of "Pilgrim Stranger."* ABE *listens, deeply moved.*)

ABE: Thank you, Miss Ann. The song moves me deeply. But I rebel against some of the words. With all my heart I rebel against them.

ANN: Why, Mr. Lincoln!

ABE: "Do not detain me, for I am going," it says. But I *want* to detain you. I don't want you to go. "I must leave you, I must leave you and be gone." No! I don't want you to leave me.

ANN (*Laughing*): I'm in no hurry right now, Mr. Lincoln.

ABE: And the refrain! It haunts me. It has haunted me ever since I first heard you sing it. "I can tarry, I can tarry but a night."

ANN (*Lightly*): It's only a song. You mustn't take it so seriously. Folks say you are a great one for telling funny stories, Mr. Lincoln, and I've seen you set the whole table a-laughing at the tavern. But tonight you seem so serious . . . about a little song. Come, tell me what it's like in the capital city of Vandalia where the Legislature meets. (*They go out, holding hands.*)

READER: In August of that year Ann Rutledge died of the fever. Abe was stunned. He sat for hours without speaking, or wandered aimlessly in the woods, gripped for the third time in his life by overwhelming grief . . . first for his mother, then for his sister Sarah, and now for Ann. But gradually time came to his rescue again, and he went back to reading law, eager to get his license to practice. (*Offstage chorus sings "Pilgrim Stranger." The voices gradually fade out.*)

As a young man of 28, Abraham Lincoln, prairie lawyer, hung up his shingle in Springfield, Illinois, which soon became the capital city. Practicing law in those days wasn't what you'd call a sit-down job. It meant spending considerable time on the road, traveling the circuit, going to towns where a short court-term was held each year.

For years Lincoln spent almost half his time on the circuit, often traveling in the company of the Judge and other lawyers. Although roads were bad, horses slow, accommodations poor along the way, and traveling wearisome, Lincoln enjoyed the trips. He liked meeting people and making new friends, spinning yarns, exchanging stories, and adding his voice to a lusty chorus. (*Offstage chorus sings "Kathleen Mavourneen" and "He Doeth All Things Well."*)

Lincoln put off marrying until he was 33 years old, and then, some folks think, he made a mighty strange choice. Mary Todd, a Kentucky belle with all the social graces, seemed an unlikely mate for a man like Abraham Lincoln who'd been brought up in a log cabin. But he married her. And folks who knew the Lincolns when they lived in Springfield said that Abe didn't always have occasion to go around with a singing heart. His wife had temperament. More than once Abe walked to the office without breakfast, picking up crackers and cheese on the way.

But he delighted in his sons—playing with them, telling them stories, indulging them, yes, and spoiling them. He would always give in to the boys when they sang his favorite song, "Jimmy Crack Corn." (*Offstage chorus sings song.*)

Lincoln went to Washington, D. C., in 1847 to serve a term in Congress. He kept his ears and eyes and mind open and the experience broadened him.

A few years later he ran for the Senate and was defeated. Then came the famous campaign of 1858 when Abraham Lincoln, the big giant, and Stephen A. Douglas, "The Little Giant," ran against each other for Senator from Illinois. Douglas had the inside track: he was already serving a term in the Senate and was running for re-election.

The two men were as different as sunflowers and roses —Lincoln tall and ungainly, Douglas short and well-groomed; Lincoln simple and unpretentious, Douglas traveling around the state in style . . . in a private railroad car, with a brass band to meet him at the station. (ABE *enters before curtain with two companions.*)

The great issue of the campaign was the extension of

slavery. Lincoln took a firm stand that the territories be free, that slavery be kept out. Douglas insisted on popular sovereignty—let the people of each territory decide. Although not an abolitionist, Lincoln did not believe in slavery, and he denounced Douglas's indifference to the right or wrong of it. The great debates went on . . .

ABE: How do you think the debates are going, boys?

1ST MAN: You have Douglas on the run, Abe. No question about it. Your "house divided" speech is being quoted all over the country.

2ND MAN (*Orating*): "A house divided against itself cannot stand. I believe this government cannot endure permanently half slave and half free." Maybe Douglas makes a bigger show, but he hasn't said anything that will go down in history like that.

1ST MAN: Folks are still chuckling over the speech you made in Springfield in July. (*Laughs*) "In my poor, lean lank face," you said, "nobody has ever seen that any cabbages were sprouting." (*Laughs*)

2ND MAN (*Laughing*): But . . . how did you put it? Oh, yes. "They have seen in Douglas's round fruitful face, post offices, land offices, marshalships and cabinet appointments . . . bursting and sprouting out in wonderful exuberance, ready to be laid hold of by their greedy hands."

1ST MAN: Somehow—don't ask me how—Douglas is able to afford a private railroad car.

ABE (*Shrugging*): As for me, boys, I wouldn't want one if our new Republican party made me a present of one. Coach or freight caboose is good enough for me, and a haywagon ride to my lodgings.

2ND MAN: What about the brass bands, though, Abe? Maybe you should go in for them. Every place we go there's three times as much trumped-up noise for Douglas as for you.

ABE: Just as a matter of taste and principle, I prefer a harmonica. (*Takes out harmonica and plays a snatch of "America."*)

2ND MAN: Why, I didn't know you played one of those things, Abe!

ABE: Fooled around with one from the time I was a kid in Indiana, since my vocal chords have never been very tuneful. Always liked the sound of a harmonica. Let Douglas have his brass bands . . . this will do for me. (*He plays "Home, Sweet Home."*)

2ND MAN: Abe! Now don't tell me not to spread the news! The harmonica is the musical instrument of the common people. You're one of them. You're for them. You speak their language. I'm going to make a point of that harmonica for the newspapers! (*They go out.*)

READER: Lincoln received the greater number of popular votes in that senatorial contest, but the State Legislature had the last word in those days, and there Douglas received the majority. Although Lincoln lost, the debates made him a figure of national importance, and the newly formed Republican party nominated him for President in 1860.

The campaign was a long one and a hard one, with Abe running against men who had long been in the public eye as governors, senators, judges. When he went East to speak, large crowds turned out to see the railsplitter, the lanky prairie lawyer who had debated so tellingly with Douglas. There were torchlight processions and noisy demonstrations . . . and brass bands. (*Band music, live or recorded, is heard in "Hail, Columbia," and "Dixie." Curtain rises on band crossing stage, if practical, with noisy campaigners shouting and carrying placards: "Abe Lincoln for President," "A Vote for Abe is a Vote for the People," "Elect the Rail-Splitter from Illinois," "Honest Abe," etc. Curtain closes.*)

Abraham Lincoln was elected President, the sixteenth President of the United States. A backwoods boy, President of the United States!

Before he left for Washington, Lincoln made a pilgrimage through the slush and cold of a late January day to a little farm near Charleston, Illinois. His father had died some years before but his stepmother was still living. (*Curtain rises on front room of a farmhouse.* SARAH BUSH LINCOLN *is sitting in a rocking chair, her head drooping over a sock she is knitting. A* YOUNG WOMAN *rushes in.*)

YOUNG WOMAN: Granny! Granny! Uncle Abe is here!

SARAH (*Waking*): Abe?

YOUNG WOMAN: Uncle Abe's come to see you, Granny.

SARAH: Busy man like Abe coming to see his old Mammy? (*Alert, excited*) Do I look all right, Sally?

YOUNG WOMAN: Hasn't anybody ever seen you frowsed-up yet? Here, let me pretty your collar a bit.

ABE (*In doorway*): Don't go fixing my best girl too pretty or I won't be able to tear myself away.

SARAH (*Starting to rise with difficulty*): Abe!

ABE (*Striding to her*): Don't you get up, Mammy. I've just come to tell you goodbye.

SARAH: What kind of way is that, Abe? Minute you get in the door you tell me you've come to say goodbye!

ABE (*Laughing*): Oh, I'm intending to sit a while first. (*Sits near her*) How've you been? And Betsy? And Tilda? And all the grandchildren? And Dennis? And Johnny's young uns?

SARAH: We're all fine, Abe . . . getting a mite older, though.

ABE: It's a way we have.

SARAH: Stand close and let me have a good look at you, son. (ABE *stands for inspection.*) You're a bit stooped. A bit tired-looking, seems like. Been working too hard, Abe?

And now you're going off to Washington and all. Oh,
I'm *that* proud of you . . . but it's a big burden they've
put on your shoulders.

ABE (*With a sigh as he sits again*): Too big, I sometimes
think.

SARAH: You can handle it, though. I never will forget those
big trees you used to chop down when you were just a
stripling. (*Chuckles*) And to think I reckoned you'd turn
out to be a writin' man. Never entered my head you'd
be President.

ABE: Nobody else thought I'd be, either, Mammy. Least of
all me.

SARAH: You still versify, Abe?

ABE: Haven't had much occasion to lately, somehow.

SARAH: Remember the lines you wrote for Jackson? You'd
just come back from that flatboat trip to New Orleans.
(*Begins to beat out tune of "Auld Lang Syne."*)

ABE: Haven't thought of that for a good long time. Let me
see if I can remember the words. (*Hesitates*)
Let auld acquaintance be forgot
And never brought to mind;
May Jackson be our President,
And Adams left behind.

SARAH: Reckon you'll have to change the words now, Abe.
I been spending considerable thought on it. Finally
worked it out.
Now Lincoln is our President,
The others left behind.

ABE (*Laughing*): So it's *you* who's turned out to be the
poet, Mammy. (*Sobering*) But I reckon now we've come
to parting it's the good old words that are best of all.
(*Singing*)
"For Auld Lang Syne, my dear,
For Auld Lang Syne;
We'll tak' a cup of kindness yet,

For Auld Lang Syne."

(*Curtain closes*)

READER: Sarah Lincoln said a cheerful goodbye to Abe, although she knew in her heart that she would never see him again.

On a rainy, cold morning in February, 1861, Lincoln left Springfield for Washington. In spite of the dreary weather, old friends had gathered at the station to say goodbye. There was even a feeble band playing "The Star-Spangled Banner." (*Offstage band music, then cheers and shouts are heard.*) Lincoln stood on the observation platform to say goodbye. (*Curtain opens on empty stage.* LINCOLN *comes in, waves.*)

ABE: My friends: No one, not in my situation, can appreciate my feeling of sadness at this parting. To this place, and the kindness of these people, I owe everything. Here I have lived a quarter of a century, and have passed from a young to an old man. Here my children have been born, and one is buried. I now leave, not knowing when or whether ever I may return . . . (*Curtain closes. The sound of a train whistle is heard offstage.*)

READER: Less than two months after Lincoln reached Washington, Fort Sumter was fired upon and the War between the States began. The house divided against itself was falling. Lincoln strained with all his strength to hold it together. Feeling sorrow rather than anger against the South for bombarding the Fort, Lincoln's one thought was to preserve the Union . . . even if a war had to be fought to do it.

Soon the capital was loud with marching feet and martial music. Lincoln's days and nights were full of anguish. On one hand he was condemned by abolitionists as being too mild, on the other by anti-abolitionists as being too harsh. A continual stream of people tried to get through to the President. (*Curtain opens on a room in the White House.* LINCOLN *is at a desk writing, piles of papers and maps in front of him.* JOHN HAY, *assistant to Lincoln's secretary, enters.*)

HAY: A Virginia lady to see you next, sir. About her son in prison.

ABE (*Wearily*): Another?

HAY: She has her young daughter with her. About the age of your boy Willie, I should say. They've been waiting a long time.

ABE: There are so many of them, Hay . . . waiting, waiting . . . pressing their wants. Warn her that I can do little, much as I might like to. (*Sighs*) Show her in. (HAY *returns with* WOMAN *and* GIRL.)

WOMAN (*Going toward desk*): Oh, Mr. President . . . now that I am face to face with you . . . (*Hesitates*) My son . . . (*Breaks down*)

ABE (*Kindly*): He is a prisoner?

WOMAN (*Nodding, handing* LINCOLN *a slip of paper*): His name . . . and the prison. He is badly wounded. (GIRL *meanwhile sees a piano and moves toward it.*)

ABE (*Looking at paper*): Eighteen years old. Wounded at the Battle of Bull Run.

WOMAN: He will die if he is kept in prison. (GIRL *sits down at piano, runs fingers over keys. Begins to play "Gentle Annie" very softly.*) Why, Lucy Belle! (GIRL *stops, embarrassed.*)

ABE: Let her be, Madam. There's little enough these days that isn't war, war, war. (*To* GIRL) Play it, sister. Do you know the words? It's a song I specially like.

GIRL (*Singing softly as she plays*):
  "Thou shall come no more, gentle Annie,
  Like a flower thy spirit did depart . . ."
  (LINCOLN *gets up and stands at the window*

as he listens. At the end of the song he turns to GIRL.)

ABE: And do you know the little song called "Twenty Years Ago"? It touches my heart above all others.

GIRL: I know it! My brother taught me. (*She plays and sings several stanzas of "Twenty Years Ago."*)

ABE (*Turning to* WOMAN *at end of song*): I shall see that your boy is released to you, Madam. Nurse him well. Have your little girl play for him. I thank her for the welcome respite she has given me from this terrible war. (WOMAN *and* GIRL *go out as curtain falls.*)

READER: The terrible war went on . . . and on. 1861. 1862. 1863. 1864. In that year Lincoln was re-elected President by a large majority who agreed with him that it was best "not to swap horses when crossing a stream." Union troops were marching to "The Battle Hymn of the Republic." (*Sound of music and marching feet off-stage, right wing.*) Confederate troops had appropriated "Dixie" as their marching song. (*Sound of music and marching feet to left offstage.*)

1865. On Sunday, April the 9th, Lee surrendered to Grant at Appomattox Court House. The Union, which Lincoln strove so hard to preserve, was saved! The Confederates were to go home, take up their work, and not fight the Government again.

Word reached Washington that night, and the next morning wild celebrating began. Bells rang, whistles blew, shouting crowds surged toward the White House to serenade the President. (*Offstage noise—shouting, singing, music.*) Lincoln finally appeared at an upstairs window of the White House. (LINCOLN *appears, holding up hand for silence. Noise dies down somewhat, but not enough for his voice to be heard.*) Most of his words of congratulation were drowned out.

ABE (*Holding up hand again for silence*): I see you have a band there.

OFFSTAGE VOICES: Three of them!

ABE: I propose now that you play a certain well-known piece of music. I thought "Dixie" one of the best tunes I ever heard. (*Shouting*) I had heard that our adversaries had attempted to appropriate it. I insisted yesterday that we had fairly captured it. (*More cheers and shouts.*) It's our tune now . . . it belongs to us all, North and South, in fellowship and unity! I ask the band to give us a good turn upon it. (*Band, offstage, or marching on, plays "Dixie." Crowd begins to sing.* LINCOLN *waves and retires. Noise dies down gradually.*)

READER: Four days later, on the night of April 14th, the President and his wife went to Ford's Theater in Washington to see a play. When the Presidential party took their seats in the box a few minutes after the curtain had gone up, the orchestra interrupted the play with the stirring music of "Hail to the Chief." Actors joined in, singing. (*A group of actors, a few men and women, stand at wings and sing several stanzas of "Hail to the Chief."*) It was the last song Abraham Lincoln ever heard. Two hours later, near the end of the play, he was shot in the head by actor John Wilkes Booth, a fanatical advocate of slavery. The next morning the President lay dead. (*Offstage chorus sings "Gentle Annie" as background.*)

Abraham Lincoln's life and work were over. A wave of grief swept from one end of the country to the other. Thousands of mourners thronged the White House and lined the route of the funeral train. Bells tolled, tears fell. In Washington, Walt Whitman, a little-known poet, poured into words his own grief and the grief that was in millions of hearts:

"My Captain does not answer, his lips are pale and still,
My father does not feel my arm, he has no pulse nor will,
The ship is anchor'd safe and sound, its voyage closed
 and done,

From fearful trip the victor ship comes in with object
    won:
Exult O shores, and ring O bells!
But I with mournful tread,
Walk the deck my Captain lies,
Fallen cold and dead."

Abraham Lincoln was dead. Yet not dead, either. For
what he stood for, what he lived by, never dies—courage,
justice, freedom, compassion, faith. One mourner put it
all in six words when he said of the martyred President:
"Now he belongs to the ages."

THE END

Sing the Songs of Springtime

Characters

Spirit of Spring	Easter
Two Harbingers	Queen of the May
April	Children
April Fool	Maypole Dancers
Arbor Day	

Time: *A spring day.*

Setting: *A meadow.*

At Rise: Spirit of Spring *comes in, looks around, and listens. Suddenly a cuckoo bird is heard offstage: "Cluck, chuck, cuckoo!"*

Spring: It's spring! It's spring! The cuckoo is calling. Where are my Harbingers? (*Sound of cuckoo from offstage again.* Spring *sings first stanza of "The Cuckoo."**)
"The cuckoo is a funny bird,
She sings as she flies.
She'll bring you glad tidings,
She'll tell you no lies.
She sips from the pretty flowers

---

* Songs marked with * can be found in *Singing Holidays*, by Oscar Brand, Knopf, N. Y., 1957. Songs marked with ** can be found in *American Music Horizons*, by McConathy et al., Silver Burdett, Morristown, N. J., 1951.

131

To make her voice clear,
And she'll never sing, 'Cuckoo,'
Till the spring of the year."
(*Offstage "Cluck, chuck, cuckoo."*)

SPRING (*Clapping hands*): Where's everyone? Come, dance and sing! It's spring.

HARBINGERS (*Dancing in*): Greetings, Spring.

SPRING: Where have you been? Haven't you broadcast the news that winter is over, that the earth is stirring with life, that the sky is bright with sun, and the cuckoo is singing?

1ST HARBINGER: We heard the first cuckoo yesterday, Spirit of Spring, and we broadcast the news far and wide. Surely April will be here in a few minutes.

2ND HARBINGER: Bringing April Fool and Arbor Day and Easter.

SPRING: Good. And what about May and June? You brought the news to them, too?

1ST HARBINGER: Yes. But you know June. She always takes her own sweet time about coming. And May— (*Hesitates*) Unfortunately the Queen of the May—

SPRING: What about the Queen of the May?

2ND HARBINGER: She has, you might say, gone into decline. She doesn't think she'll be able to come to the reunion. She's hobbling around with a cane.

SPRING: A cane!

1ST HARBINGER: The poor Queen has been having a hard time.

SPRING: That will never do! Spring is the time to dance and sing. We can't have May limping around. Why, see how brightly the sun shines, how the puddles sparkle, how the buds glisten, how the birds sing! (*Offstage "Cluck, chuck, cuckoo."*) It won't do for the Queen of the May to be under the weather when so much depends on her.

OFFSTAGE VOICES (*Singing "Spring Carol"**):

"Spring is here with all her joys,
    Serving to remind us
Summer days will follow soon,
    Winter lies behind us."

(APRIL, APRIL FOOL, ARBOR DAY, EASTER *dance in, singing.
*   *They join hands with* SPRING *and* HARBINGERS *and circle
around, singing the second stanza of "Spring Carol."*)

ALL:

"Flowers show their tender buds,
    Lightly colored petals
Beckon, as the gentle breeze
    On the meadow settles." (*Etc.*)

SPRING: Welcome, welcome, my dear friends. It's wonderful to see you after such a long, cold, lonesome winter.
April, you always remind us of rhymes—flowers and
showers, buds and floods, roots and boots . . .

OTHERS: And bumbershoots!

SPRING (*Laughing*): Yes, bumbershoots. What do you have
to say for yourself, April?

APRIL: I never seem to be able to make up my mind. Folks
say I blow hot or cold at the drop of a hat. April Fool is
going to speak for me this year.

APRIL FOOL: I'm perfectly willing to speak, but don't ask
me to sing with this *frog* in my throat. (*Takes stance
and recites*)

April, April, aren't you queer,
    April, aren't you funny?
You pout and weep and shed a tear,
    Then smile and look all sunny!
Now you send a warming breeze . . .
    Now your breeze is cooling . . .
April, April, you're a tease,
    You're always April-fooling!

OTHERS:

April, April, you're a tease,

You're always April-fooling!

SPRING (*Looking around*): Let's see who else is here for our spring reunion. Ah, Arbor Day. We're always glad to see you. (ARBOR DAY *curtsies.*) You've made such a difference in America. Why, a hundred years ago when pioneers were moving west, some of the prairie states had hardly any trees at all. Now, thanks to you, millions of trees are growing on the prairies, holding moisture in the soil, breaking the wind, making America beautiful. What do you have to say to us, Arbor Day?

ARBOR DAY: Just what I've always been saying . . . in three words. Trees. Trees. Trees. (*Begins to sing "The Tree in the Wood"* *:)
"All in the wood there was a tree,
The prettiest tree that you ever did see.
And the green grass grew all around, all around,"

ALL:
"And the green grass grew all around."

ARBOR DAY:
"And on that tree there was a branch,
The prettiest branch that you ever did see.
Branch on the tree,
And the tree in the wood
And the green grass grew all around, all around,"

ALL:
"And the green grass grew all around."

(*This song can keep going as long as desired with the addition of a nest, an egg in the nest, a bird on the egg, a feather on the bird, etc.*)

SPRING: All that because there was a tree!

ARBOR DAY: Trees. Trees. Trees.

APRIL: We should remember to ask Johnny Appleseed to come join us some time. He was one of the greatest planters of trees in America. Apple trees. He went all over Ohio in the early days, and even into Kentucky and

Indiana, planting orchards for the new settlers, making the wilderness look more like home. He'll always be remembered.

APRIL FOOL (*Cavorting around*):
Oh, planting trees on Arbor Day
Is fine, we are agreed,
But *every* day was Arbor Day
For Johnny Appleseed!

1ST HARBINGER: There's no April Fool about that.

SPRING: And here's Easter, to remind us of the triumph of life after winter's long sleep, to speak to us of renewal, and rebirth, and joy in living. What's your message this year, Easter?

EASTER (*Swinging into the spiritual, "That Great Getting-Up Morning"* *:)
"Come and let me tell you 'bout the rising of the Saviour,
Fare thee well, fare thee well, (*Etc.*)
On that great getting-up morning
Fare thee well, fare thee well." (*Etc.*)

SPRING: I always marvel at how young you look, Easter. And you've been in the world such a long time.

EASTER: Isn't everything young in spring—fresh and new and eager?

SPRING: Everything should be. But . . . accidents do happen. (*Looks around*) The Queen of the May hasn't come, has she? Harbingers, run tell her we're waiting for her, we need her. What's spring without the May Queen? Tell her our reunion simply won't be complete without her. Tell her to come, cane and all. (HARBINGERS *run out.*)

APRIL FOOL: Cane and all?

EASTER: Is something wrong with the Queen of the May?

ARBOR DAY: When did it happen?

SPRING: She's gone into decline, they tell me. She's not like her old self at all.

EASTER: But how *can* anything be wrong? May is a month of joy and gladness, a time of wonder and surprises, quite as much as April. Remember how she always used to come in singing "The May Carol?"

APRIL FOOL (*Dancing around, mimicking*): Yes. Hand me my crown, Arbor Day. (*Gives* ARBOR DAY *his fool's cap and puts on garland, half singing and half chanting "The May Carol."* *)

"This morning is the month of May,
The finest of the year.
Good people all, both great and small,
I wish you joyful cheer."

OTHERS (*Joining in*):
"I've wandered far, through all the night,
And also through the day.
And when I come your way again,
I'll bring a branch of may."

SPRING: I doubt if she'll sing it this year.

EASTER: Poor May, whatever is the trouble?

APRIL FOOL (*Looking toward wings*): Shall I help fetch her? (*He has put his fool's cap back on.*)

SPRING: No. She might think we're fooling if she sees you, April Fool, and this is a serious matter.

ARBOR DAY: I remember the Queen used to love the rousing old English country songs. Perhaps if we sang one it would encourage her. What about "Hey Ho to the Greenwood"?

SPRING: To the greenwood let us go!

APRIL FOOL (*Peering out wings*): Here she comes. And she's not singing her May carol.

EASTER: She's hobbling along with a cane.

SPRING: Come on, let's give her a rousing welcome . . . three cheers and a song.

ALL: Hooray, hooray, hooray, for the beautiful Queen of the May! (SPRING *leads the singing of "Hey Ho to the Greenwood."* **)

"Hey ho, to the greenwood now let us go,
Sing heave—and ho,
And there shall we find both buck and doe,
Sing heave—and ho . . ." (*Etc.*)

(QUEEN OF THE MAY *hobbles in with cane, a* HARBINGER
on each side.)

SPRING (*Hurrying up*): What in the world has happened to
you, my dear? Did you have a fall?

QUEEN: A fall? Well, yes, you might put it that way.

SPRING: It's the first time you haven't come singing your
carol.

QUEEN (*Sighing*): I haven't felt much like singing lately.
(*Takes out handkerchief*) Nobody loves me any more.

EASTER: Why, what do you mean—nobody loves you? We
all do.

QUEEN: I mean . . . I mean nobody else does. In olden
times in England I really *was* somebody. May Day was
the great public holiday of spring.

APRIL FOOL: Nobody ever made a holiday of me, but I
have a lot of fun slipping in edgewise.

QUEEN: People used to get up early on the first day of May
to gather flowers and branches, and to dance and sing.
They carried the Maypole to the village green and set
it up with great ceremony and danced around it. Now
who remembers May Day and the Queen of the May?
Where are the dancers? The garlands? The Maypoles?
The ribbons? (*Wipes her eyes*) Nobody remembers me
any more.

SPRING: Oh, I'm sure many people remember you.

OTHERS: We do! (SPRING *beckons to* HARBINGERS, *whispers
to them. They smile and nod and go out.*)

QUEEN: Ever since the time of the Pilgrims, I've been out
of things. Maybe you don't remember, but when the
people of Plymouth town set up the first Maypole to
celebrate spring, the Pilgrim fathers made them take it
right down. They didn't believe in dancing, or fun, or

having May games or Maypoles. They didn't believe in *me*.

EASTER: It doesn't seem possible.

QUEEN: I'm not saying they weren't good and upright and all, as they looked at things. But they never made me welcome among them. I never really had a chance to get a foothold in America. And time doesn't seem to improve matters. (*Wipes her eyes*) Oh, the beautiful flowers and streamers of old England! Now no one cares if I remember how to dance and sing or not.

SPRING: Come, come, my dear, it can't be as bad as that.

QUEEN: May Day just isn't important any more. (*There is the sound of singing offstage.* QUEEN *is suddenly alert.*) Why, that's my song! "The May Carol."

SPRING: So it is.

QUEEN: I didn't think anyone remembered . . .

CHILDREN (*Running in with May baskets, singing*):
  "This morning is the month of May,
  The finest of the year.
  Good people all, both great and small,
  We wish you joyful cheer."

(*They curtsy to* QUEEN, SPRING, *etc., in turn.*)

SPRING: What do you have in your baskets, may I ask?

CHILDREN: Mayflowers.

BOY: We got up early to pick them, so we wouldn't be late for school.

QUEEN (*Hopefully*): And are you going to make a garland for a Maypole?

GIRL: No. We're going to hang our baskets on doorknobs when nobody's looking. Then we'll ring the bell and run away. Whoever comes to the door will be surprised to see it's May Day.

QUEEN: What a charming idea! (*Steps forward eagerly to look into baskets and forgets her cane.* APRIL FOOL *catches it just in time to keep it from falling.*) Mayflowers. Spring beauties. Daffodils. Cherry blossoms. Apple bloom. Candytuft. And how did you get this delightful idea for May Day?

GIRL: Why, we do it every year in our town.

BOY: Doesn't everybody? It's fun. You have to be quick, I tell you, after ringing a doorbell, so you won't be found out.

GIRL: And people are always so surprised to get a May basket.

QUEEN: Well, I should think so. I would be, too.

GIRL: Doesn't everybody do it on the first of May?

QUEEN: I'm afraid not. (*She sighs, then suddenly remembers her cane. Takes it from* APRIL FOOL.)

CHILDREN: They *should.* (*They skip out singing "The May Carol."*)

SPRING: There, my dear, you see everyone hasn't forgotten May Day. (HARBINGERS *come running in.*)

HARBINGERS: Make way! Make way!

SPRING: What is it, Harbingers?

HARBINGERS: Something we found in the park, in the first park we came to. Make way! (*They wave everyone toward back of stage.*)

1ST HARBINGER: They were one dancer short, so we told them to come here.

QUEEN: Who were?

APRIL FOOL (*Stepping up*): If they're one dancer short, what about me? *I'm* short. (SPRING *waves him aside.*) I can dance and sing. (*He ducks under* SPRING'S *arm and prances forward, singing fifth stanza of " 'Twas May Day in the Morning." **)

"There was a man who grew so fat
He always stuck in his rocking chair,
It doesn't rhyme but I don't care—
'Twas May Day in the morning."

(*Others laugh and push him aside as* DANCERS *enter carry-*

ing a Maypole and singing, "Now Is the Month of May-ing." **)

DANCERS:

"Now is the month of maying,
When merry lads are playing,
Fa la la, (*Etc.*)
Each with his bonny lass,
A-dancing on the grass.
Fa la la . . ." (*Etc.*)

QUEEN: That's one of the songs they used to sing in England years ago! (*She is much excited.*) Where did you learn it? Where did you come across it?

1ST DANCER: Why, it's in one of our songbooks at school—plain as day.

2ND DANCER: If we had one more dancer, we'd do an English country dance, and then weave the Maypole.

3RD DANCER: That's in our songbook, too.

4TH DANCER: But we're one dancer short.

QUEEN: One dancer short! (*She drops her cane as she steps forward eagerly.* APRIL FOOL *catches cane just in time.*) Would I do? I know the song. I know all the May Day songs and dances.

DANCERS: You *do*!

5TH DANCER: Then you're just the one we need.

SPRING: It's spring, it's spring. Come, dance and sing! (QUEEN *joins dancers, and they quickly set up the Maypole. It may be placed in a strong Christmas tree holder. As they sing "Now Is the Month of Maying," they go into the dance outlined on page 143 of "American Music Horizons." Music continues until weaving of Maypole is completed.* QUEEN OF THE MAY *dances gaily.*)

SPRING (*Rushing up at end of song*): My dear, are you all right? After all that dancing and exertion?

DANCERS: She's wonderful—and she didn't even practice!

QUEEN: I haven't felt so good in years. Not since the seventeenth century. I'm so excited to know that these things are going on in America.

1st DANCER: Miss . . . Miss . . . we would like to crown you Queen of the May and have you as guest of honor at our school program this afternoon. May we?

OTHERS (*Amused*): The Queen of the May! The Queen of the May!

SPRING (*Laughing*): Do you think you could fill the role, my dear?

QUEEN (*Laughing*): I could try.

APRIL FOOL: Who's fooling now?

2ND DANCER (*Urgently*): Will you be our May Queen, please? (APRIL FOOL *mischievously bows before* QUEEN, *and holds out cane to her.*)

QUEEN: Be done with your fooling. What do I want with a cane! (*She does a little dance.*) Don't you know it's spring, when everything is young and gay?

1st DANCER: Then you *will* be our May Queen?

QUEEN: Be your May Queen? Indeed I will, dear friends. There's nothing in the whole wide world I'd rather be. (*All sing "Now Is the Month of Maying" as the curtain falls.*)

THE END

Sing the Songs of Travel

Characters

TRAVEL AGENT	JERRY
JACK	PHYLLIS
DAISY	OSCAR
PETER	POLICEMAN
MARGIE	BOSS OF TRAVEL BUREAU
PROFESSOR	

SETTING: *A Travel Bureau booth stands at one side of the stage. There is a sign on front which reads: "Business as Usual—Make Your Travel Plans Here." At the back of the stage is a bench.*

AT RISE: TRAVEL AGENT *is tinkering with gong as he stands in booth. He smiles as he taps it lightly and it rings. He takes cardboard from under counter and prints on it with red crayon, then fastens it over "Business as Usual," so the sign reads: "Special Today! Make Your Travel Plans Here."*

AGENT (*Calling out*):
Special today!

Note: Words and music to songs for this play may be found in *The Fireside Book of Favorite American Songs,* by Boni and Lloyd, Simon and Schuster, New York, 1952; *The Fireside Book of Folk Songs,* Boni and Lloyd, Simon and Schuster, New York, 1947; *Singing Juniors,* by Pitts, Glenn, Watters and Wersten, Ginn and Co., Boston, 1953. In most cases, any appropriate songs may be substituted for the ones suggested here.

You can't go wrong.
Have a wonderful ride
For just a song!
Will you ride on a horse?
Will you sail the seas?
Will you fly like a bird
Up over the trees?
(JACK *and* DAISY *enter, stand at wings listening.*)
Special, my friends!
At the sound of the gong
You can go on a trip
For just a song! (*Taps gong loudly.* JACK *and* DAISY *go to booth.*)

JACK: Do you mean we can travel . . . for nothing?

AGENT: For a song.

DAISY: What kind of song?

AGENT: That depends on the kind of ride you want. (JACK *and* DAISY *confer.*)

JACK: I'd like a bicycle ride, and so would Daisy.

AGENT: That shouldn't be too difficult. (*Looks through some sheets of music on the counter, picks one out.*) This was a pretty famous song in its day, sixty or seventy years ago. Sing it and see. (*He hands* JACK *the sheet.*) A ride for a song! Try the third stanza. (JACK *and* DAISY *look at music, then* JACK *begins to sing "Daisy Bell"*)

JACK:
"I will stand by you in 'wheel' or woe,
Daisy, Daisy!
You'll be the bell(e) which I'll ring, you know!
Sweet little Daisy Bell!"
(AGENT *slips out to get a bicycle, bringing it in while the song is still in progress. It is an old bike with an extra seat and set of handlebars.*)
"You'll take the 'lead' in each 'trip' we take,
Then, if I don't do well,

I will permit you to use the brake,
My beautiful Daisy Bell!"

AGENT: Voice up on the chorus, boy!
That's where the bicycle comes in.

JACK (*Having a good time*):
"Daisy, Daisy,
Give me your answer true!
I'm half crazy,
All for the love of you!
It won't be a stylish marriage,
I can't afford a carriage,
But you'll look sweet
Upon the seat
Of a bicycle built for two!"
(*He bows deeply to* DAISY *and the* AGENT.)

AGENT: Won't she look sweet, though! This bicycle will do
the trick. (DAISY *and* JACK *stand on either side of the
bicycle, each holding a set of handlebars. With* AGENT's
help, JACK *makes several attempts to get going. Finally
they "ride" around, holding up the bike.* AGENT *sings.*)
"You look sweet
Upon the seat
Of a bicycle built for two."
(*They finish the ride, laughing merrily.*)

DAISY: Well, I never had a ride for a song before.

JACK: It certainly was special! (*They start to go out.*
AGENT *calls after them.*)

AGENT:
Why don't you stay and watch the fun?
Our trips for a song have just begun.

JACK: Thanks. Maybe we will. (*He and* DAISY *sit on bench.*
AGENT *removes bicycle, returns to chant.*)

AGENT:
Special, my friends!
Come right along.

Travel today
For just a song . . .
At the sound of the gong! (*Rings gong loudly.* PETER *has come in during the chant. He approaches the booth.*)

PETER: Travel—for a song?

AGENT: That's right. What kind of travel do you have in mind?

PETER: Well, I've ridden in a car, of course, hundreds of times. And I've ridden horseback at my aunt's farm. And I've ridden in a plane . . . twice. And on a boat across Lake Michigan. And I've ridden on my uncle's tractor. But I've never had any first-hand experience with a train.

AGENT: A train! Let me see . . . (*Looks through music sheets*) What about "The Wabash Cannon Ball"? That's a famous one. When railroads first spread across the country, people got so excited they used to sing about them . . . about the noise and speed and all. (*Hands sheet to* PETER) Sing your song and I'll see that you get some first-hand experience with a train.

PETER (*Singing second stanza*):
    "There is music in her jingle,
    There is music in her roar,
    Like a will-o'-the-wisp she travels,
    On her way from shore to shore.
    May her greatness last forever,
    May the glory never fall,
    Of the Western Combination,
    Of the Wabash Cannon Ball."
    (*While he sings,* AGENT *brings in track and electric train which he plugs in at one side of stage. He soon has the train going.*)

AGENT: The Wabash Cannon Ball! All aboard!

PETER (*Down on his knees, admiring train*): Caboose and everything!

AGENT (*Singing part of first stanza*):

"She's graceful as a comet,
Smoother than a waterfall,
It's the Western Combination,
It's the Wabash Cannon Ball."
(JACK *and* DAISY *enter into the singing.*)

JACK *and* DAISY:
"She'll be comin' round the mountain when she comes,
She'll be comin' round the mountain when she comes
. . ." (*Etc.*)

AGENT: Won't she, though? That's what the work gangs on the railroads used to sing seventy years ago. Well, I'd better get back to business. (*Calls out, while* PETER *continues to play with train.*)
Will you ride in a car
Or a boat you can paddle?
Will you climb on a horse
And straddle a saddle?
(MARGIE *comes in, stands listening.*)
Special today!
For just a song
You can have a good ride
At the sound of the gong.
(*Clangs gong*)

MARGIE: Are you fooling?

AGENT: I should say not. Not *today*. Do you have a secret yearning for a very special ride?

MARGIE: Yes, I do. But it's so out of style, I don't think I'll ever get it.

AGENT: Nothing's out of style around here. What do you have in mind?

MARGIE: I'd dearly love to ride in a one-horse open sleigh. But there aren't any. (*Sighs*)

AGENT (*Confidentially*): Today is special. A one-horse open sleigh? (*Looks through music*) Here you are . . . for a song. (*Hands her a sheet*) Sing it.

MARGIE: Oh, I know this one! (*Begins to sing "Jingle Bells"*)

"Dashing through the snow
In a one-horse open sleigh . . ." (*Etc.*)

(*As she sings, AGENT brings in sled mounted on roller skates. He also brings a string of bells. Joins MARGIE in chorus, while getting her settled on the sled.*)

MARGIE *and* AGENT:
"Jingle bells! Jingle bells!
Jingle all the way!
Oh, what fun it is to ride
In a one-horse open sleigh."

AGENT: I'm the horse. Let's go! (*He pulls her around the stage, shaking the bells while they repeat the chorus.*)

MARGIE: That was wonderful. Do you have specials like this very often?

AGENT: This is the first time. I just thought of it last night when I changed the tone of the gong. (*Looks around furtively*) Don't tell the boss. Business has been rather slow . . . and . . . well, I thought I'd liven it up a bit.

MARGIE: I won't tell.

AGENT:
Stick around and watch the fun.
Our bargain trips have just begun.

(*MARGIE goes to bench, stopping to watch PETER and train on the way. AGENT removes sled and bells, returns to resume chant as an absent-minded PROFESSOR crosses stage.*)

Have a wonderful ride
For just a song!
Special today
At the sound of the gong. (*He clangs the gong so hard it startles the PROFESSOR.*)

PROFESSOR: Eh? (*Looks around*)

AGENT:

A wonderful ride

For just a song.

PROFESSOR: You aren't trying to take me for a ride, are you?

AGENT: For just a song.

PROFESSOR: Unheard of.

AGENT: Ask the folks around here.

CHILDREN: He's right. You can't go wrong.

AGENT: What kind of ride would you like, Professor?

PROFESSOR: To tell the truth . . . (*Looks around, somewhat embarrassed*) I've always had a secret ambition . . . to be a cowboy.

JACK *and* PETER: Whoopee, ti-yi-yo!

PROFESSOR: But never in all my life have I had a chance to ride a horse.

AGENT: And now you can ride one for a song! (*Looks through music*) Professor, you're in luck. (*Hands him a sheet*) Here you are . . . sing it.

PROFESSOR (*Hesitating*): I'm not very good at singing.

AGENT: Oh, a simple song like that . . . come on!

PROFESSOR (*Singing "Song of the Saddle" with vim but more or less out of tune*):

"Ridin' down the canyon road,

Headin' for my own abode . . ."

(*Looks up questioningly*)

AGENT: You're doing fine, Professor. Keep going. (*As PROFESSOR finishes first stanza, AGENT goes to wings for broomstick horse.*)

PROFESSOR (*Finishing*): What's *that*?

AGENT: Your horse, sir.

PROFESSOR: What do I do with it?

AGENT: Ride it . . . like this. (*Straddles broomstick and gallops absurdly around stage and back to PROFESSOR*)

PROFESSOR: Oh, I say . . . what fun! (*He mounts the steed*

and goes right off the stage. Others laugh and sing "The Old Gray Mare.")

AGENT *(At end of song)*: Well, I mustn't neglect my work. *(Goes back to booth and chants as* JERRY *and* PHYLLIS *enter)*

Come one, come all,
You can't go wrong.
Travel in state
For just a song
At the sound of the gong. *(Clangs gong.* JERRY *and* PHYLLIS *go to booth.)*

PHYLLIS: But, you see, we don't want to travel in state.

JERRY: Anything but.

PHYLLIS: We want to ride in a hay wagon on a hayride party. But since we live in a city, we never get a chance.

AGENT: You've come to the right place at the right time. We supply all kinds of rides today, for a song. *(*JERRY *and* PHYLLIS *look at each other, puzzled.)* Let's see now . . . wagon. That'll be under the W's. *(Looks through music, picks out sheet, hands it to* JERRY*)* Here you are. Sing it, my boy, while you wait for the wagon!

JERRY *(Singing "Wait for the Wagon")*:
"Will you come with me, my Phyllis dear,
To yon blue mountain free?
Where blossoms smell the sweetest,
Come, rove along with me."
*(*AGENT *goes out for wagon, all on stage join in chorus.)*

ALL:
"Wait for the wagon,
Wait for the wagon,
Wait for the wagon and we'll all take a ride." *(*AGENT *brings in delivery boy's wagon full of hay.)*

AGENT: Here we are, folks, all set for a hayride. Climb in! *(All gather around the wagon.* PHYLLIS *and* JERRY *get in and others join them.* PETER *helps* AGENT *pull wagon around stage, as all repeat chorus.*)

JERRY (*At end of song, picking hay from sweater*): It tickles. All that for a song!

PHYLLIS: You even have some hay in your hair, Jerry. (*Picks it out*) Now nobody can say we've never been on a hayride. (*They start out, laughing. Others go back to places.*)

AGENT (*Removing wagon, over his shoulder*):
Why not stay and watch the fun?
Our special day is far from done.
(JERRY *and* PHYLLIS *go to bench.* AGENT *comes back and takes up chant.*)
Special today!
At the sound of the gong
You can take a trip
For just a song. (OSCAR *comes in.* AGENT *forgets to ring gong.*)

OSCAR: What's the catch?

AGENT: No catch. You travel for a song.

OSCAR: Travel where?

AGENT: Take your choice. You start right here at the Travel Bureau.

OSCAR: Couldn't start here the way *I* want to travel.

AGENT: What way is that?

OSCAR: I want to row a boat. Where's the water?

AGENT: Little thing like that! Today we don't have to worry about minor details. So you want to row a boat. (*Looks through music, finds a sheet, hands it to* OSCAR) Here you go. Sing it.

OSCAR: What for?

AGENT: For your boat ride.

OSCAR: Say . . . you can't fool me. I'm not going to make a fool of myself when there's no water to row a boat

on. I'm going to get the police after you, that's what.
You're a fake. (*He stalks out.*)

AGENT: That boy needs a paddle instead of an oar! (*Stops
short*) Oh, oh! I forgot to ring the gong. The magic gong
that makes everyone merry. I forgot to ring it . . . that's
the trouble. Poor boy, he wanted to row a boat. (*Goes
to gong and taps it*)

PHYLLIS *and* JERRY (*Singing*):
"Row, row, row your boat
Gently down the stream,
Merrily, merrily, merrily, merrily,
Life is but a dream."
(*Others join in at intervals, to make a three-part round.
In the midst of the singing,* OSCAR *comes back with a*
POLICEMAN.)

POLICEMAN: What's going on here? Life is but a dream,
is it? Not when you're in business, it isn't. (*To* AGENT)
What's this dream of rowing a boat without water? What
do you charge for such nonsense?

AGENT: Only a song, sir.

POLICEMAN: A song!

AGENT: That's all. An innocent little song.

POLICEMAN (*To* OSCAR): I can't arrest anybody when he's
not asking for money. If he wants to do business for a
song, that's *his* business.

AGENT (*To* POLICEMAN):
Take a ride for a song
At the sound of the gong. (*He sounds gong loudly, and
it skids to the floor. He picks it up, shakes it, puts it back
on counter.*) Have you a hidden yearning for a certain
kind of ride, sir?

POLICEMAN: That I have. But it's all foolishness, and I
know it full well.

AGENT: What's all foolishness?

POLICEMAN: I . . . well, I never wanted to *row* a boat, like Oscar here. But I've always had a hankering to be a sailor . . . on one of those square-riggers, you know, with mains'l and tops'l and all. But, as I say, it's all foolishness with hardly a square-rigger left on the high seas.

AGENT: Nothing's foolishness at *this* Travel Bureau, my man. (*Looks through music, picks out sheet*) Do you know what a bowline is?

POLICEMAN: Why, that'd be the rope fastened near the middle of the leech of a square sail, to keep the weather edge taut forward when a ship's close-hauled.

AGENT (*Amazed*): Anybody who knows that much about a square-rigger certainly deserves to ride on one. You've come to the right place, sir. Here's your song. You'll probably need Oscar's help. (*He taps gong as he goes out for rope.* POLICEMAN *and* OSCAR *look over the song.* AGENT *comes back with stout rope, one end of which is held offstage so it can't be pulled too easily.* AGENT *tosses rope to* POLICEMAN.) Here's your bowline . . . all for a song. Brace yourselves, there. The ship's pitching. Pull together now, to hoist that water-soaked mains'l. Haul away!

POLICEMAN *and* OSCAR (*Pulling on rope as they sing "Haul Away, Joe"*):
"Way, haul away, we'll haul away the bowlin'
Way, haul away, we'll haul away, Joe . . ." (*On the word "Joe" they give an extra-hard pull. They repeat stanza. Then* PETER, JACK, DAISY, MARGIE, JERRY *and* PHYLLIS *join in the fun by singing "Sailing, sailing, over the bounding main," etc.* POLICEMAN *and* OSCAR *continue to pull on rope.* BOSS *suddenly strides in. He is astonished. He goes to booth and tries to ring gong for attention. It doesn't work. Pounds fist on counter.*)

BOSS: What's the matter with everyone? Stop! Look! Listen!

I've been trying to make myself heard, but the gong is broken.

AGENT: Broken!

BOSS: What's going on? (POLICEMAN, *embarrassed, tries to tiptoe to wings. The* BOSS *calls to* POLICEMAN.) Just a minute there. (POLICEMAN *turns back.*)

AGENT: There's nothing to get excited about, sir. It's just a little publicity stunt to drum up some business, you see. (*Nods at group*) I'm sure none of them will ever forget our agency.

ALL: Never!

BOSS: Well, *that's* good. But enough is enough. (*Strides to booth and takes down "Special Today" sign, so "Business as Usual" shows again.*) Now then, let's get back to business. (AGENT *takes his place behind the counter.* JACK *and* DAISY *go out singing chorus of "Daisy Bell."* PETER *goes out singing chorus of "The Wabash Cannon Ball."* MARGIE *goes out singing chorus of "Jingle Bells."* JERRY *and* PHYLLIS *go out singing chorus of "Wait for the Wagon."* OSCAR *goes out singing "Row, Row, Row Your Boat."* POLICEMAN *goes out singing "Sailing, Sailing."*) Now that your *publicity* has left, we can tend to business . . . as usual. (*He strides impatiently up and down the stage, looking expectantly toward the wings. No business is in sight.*) *What* business?

AGENT: That's just it, sir. (*He tinkers with gong.*)

BOSS: What's just it?

AGENT: The gong seems to have broken. It helped liven things up.

BOSS: It did?

AGENT: Decidedly. It put people in a good mood, a very good mood.

BOSS: Then, for goodness' sake, fix it. I'll give you time off right now to go and fix it.

AGENT (*Gleefully picking up gong*): Thank you, sir. I
know just what it needs. (*He goes out singing*)
"Merrily, merrily, merrily, merrily,
Life is but a dream." (*Curtain*)

THE END

Sing the Songs of Cowboys

Characters

MAN
LARRY
STEVE
MILLIE
MORTON
OTHER BOYS AND GIRLS
RILEY COCHRAN (THE BOSS)
BILLY
SPIKE
TWO TRAIL JUMPERS
TWO LINE MEN

SETTING: *An empty stage, except for a park bench left.*
AT RISE: *A white-haired* MAN *is sitting on the park bench, reading a newspaper.* BOYS *and* GIRLS *wearing cowboy outfits run in.* BOYS *are playfully trying to lasso the* GIRLS *while singing the first stanza of "Whoopee, Ti-Yi-Yo."*

BOYS (*Swinging into refrain of song*):
  "Whoopee ti-yi-yo, git along little dogies,
  For you know that Wyoming'll be your new home (*Etc.*)"
STEVE (*Throwing lariat toward* MILLIE): Almost caught one. Git along, little dogie.

Most of the songs in this play can be found in *Best Loved American Songs,* by John and Alan Lomax, Grosset & Dunlap, New York, 1947; and in *Cowboy Songs and Other Frontier Ballads,* by John and Alan Lomax, Macmillan, New York, 1938.

MILLIE: Larry, are you going to stand there and let Steve call your sister names?

LARRY: Nobody's calling you names, Millie.

MORTON: A dogie's a perfectly nice little motherless calf.

MILLIE: Me—a calf?

GIRLS: Us—calves! (*They turn on* BOYS *and chase them around the stage.*) Git along, little dogies! (*Sing second stanza of "Whoopee, Ti-Yi-Yo."*)

"It's early in spring we round up the dogies;

We mark them and brand them and bob off their tails . . . ." (*Etc.*)

MILLIE: Watch it, Morton, or you'll have a rope around your neck! (*She aims playfully at* MORTON, *but misses him.* BOYS *laughingly join in refrain of song.*)

LARRY: Boy, those were the days! Cowboy days. Days on the cattle trail.

STEVE: Where never was heard a discouraging word and the skies were not cloudy all day.

LARRY: And the moon swept the sky at night. (*He plays a guitar or twirls his lariat as he sings the first two stanzas of "The Cowboy's Dream."*)

"Last night as I lay on the prairie

And look'd at the stars in the sky . . ." (*Etc.*)

(BOYS *and* GIRLS *join in refrain of song, moving around stage as they sing.*)

ALL:

"Roll on, roll on, roll on, little dogies . . ." (*Etc.*)

LARRY:

"They say there will be a great round-up,

And cowboys, like dogies, will stand . . ." (*Etc.*)

ALL: "Roll on, roll on, roll on, little dogies . . ." (*Etc.*)

STEVE: Wish we could turn the clock back to the good old cowboy days.

MORTON: Let's see . . . that would be between 1870 and
1890. The great age of cowpunching!

STEVE: I don't know when it was . . . all I know is the
sky was the limit, the big blue sky over the plains from
horizon to horizon . . . and no barbed wire fences
standing in the way. Wish I could have been riding into
Cheyenne on one of the cattle drives. Boy, Cheyenne!
The town was wide open and exciting in the old days.

MORTON: Especially in the '70's, after the railroad came.

LARRY: You can have Cheyenne, Steve. Montana for me!
Give me the wild and woolly west of Montana. (*Swings
rope and begins to sing "Good-bye, Old Paint, I'm
a-leavin' Cheyenne."*)
"Good-bye, Old Paint, I'm a-leavin' Cheyenne . . ."
   (*Etc.*)

MILLIE (*Joining in*):
"I'm off for Montana,
Good-bye, Old Paint, I'm a-leavin' Cheyenne."

MORTON: While you're in the wishing business, why don't
you wish you could ride up the Old Chisholm Trail behind a herd of longhorns . . . on the most famous trail
there was? It stretched more than six hundred miles,
from San Antonio, Texas, through Oklahoma, to the
railroad yards at Dodge City and Abilene, Kansas.
(*Turns to* MILLIE) Millie, how many half-wild longhorns
do you think were driven up the Old Chisholm Trail,
anyway?

MILLIE: I haven't the faintest idea. But *one* half-wild longhorn, with huge spreading horns, would be enough for
me. More than enough.

LARRY: How many, Morton?

MORTON: Between 1870 and 1890 at least twelve million
cattle went up the Chisholm Trail. And about a million
mustang ponies, besides.

STEVE: That's a lot of livestock! No wonder the trail was famous.

MORTON: There'd be two or three thousand cattle in a herd usually, and cowboys on the trail for months.

LARRY: That's the life . . . to be on the trail for months! No wonder they used to sing about it. Come on, Steve. (*They begin to sing "The Old Chisholm Trail," taking alternate stanzas, with other* BOYS *joining in refrain.*)

STEVE:

"Come along, boys, and listen to my tale,
I'll tell you of my troubles on the Old Chisholm Trail
. . . " (*Etc.*)

LARRY (*After a number of stanzas*): It goes on and on . . . like the old trail itself. I read that one cowboy could sing sixty-nine verses without stopping . . . about everything that happened along the way, in all kinds of weather.

MILLIE: Why did they call it the Chisholm Trail?

STEVE: You've got me. (*Looks at others questioningly*) Morton, you know all the answers.

MORTON (*Hesitating*): It's . . . it's probably named after some famous old cowboy.

MAN (*On bench*): You're wrong there, Bud! (BOYS *and* GIRLS *turn to look at* MAN *in astonishment.*)

MORTON: What?

MAN: Said you're wrong about the Chisholm Trail being named after a cowboy. (BOYS *and* GIRLS *edge closer, curious.*)

MAN: Named after a half-breed Cherokee Indian trader, it was.

MORTON: It was?

MAN: Cherokee trader, name of Jesse Chisholm. Oklahoma was Indian Territory back in those days, you know. Jesse Chisholm broke the trail in the spring of 1866 when he drove his wagon of buffalo hides through to a trading post in Wichita, Kansas. Cowboys came after, following his wagon trail. Reckon I ought to know. I'm from out that-a-way.

LARRY: You are! (BOYS *and* GIRLS *move closer.*)

MAN: Couldn't help hearing you say you'd like to turn the clock back.

BOYS: Yes, *sir.*

STEVE: You see, there's not much chance to be a good old-fashioned cowboy these days. It's not the way it used to be.

MORTON: When the range was open from Texas to Montana, and east to the Dakotas and west to Idaho.

STEVE: Now everything's fenced in, and you don't have to drive cows very far because trucks and railroads go everywhere.

MAN: Right. But it wasn't all glamor being a cowboy on one of the old cattle trails, let me tell you. Got to be pretty monotonous after a week or two . . . lonesome, dusty, hot, flies and gnats buzzing around. 'Twas a dreary life in many ways.

BOYS: Dreary!

MAN: I notice there's one song you didn't sing . . . wonder if I can recollect it. (*Starts to sing, tentatively at first, then stronger and with feeling, "The Dreary, Dreary Life."*)

"A cowboy's life is a dreary, dreary life,
Some say it's free from care
Rounding up the cattle from morning till night
In the middle of the prairie so bare . . ." (*Etc.*)

STEVE (*At end of song*): All I can say is . . . it's the kind of life I'd like to live.

MAN: I don't know about that. The cattle trail's not nearly as exciting as trails you folks can follow these days. Trails into space and the like. Times change. One trail goes out, and another opens to take its place. I recollect something about the Old Chisholm Trail that might make you see it wasn't all a bed o' roses . . . if you've time to listen.

BOYS *and* GIRLS: Yes, yes!

MAN: Happened back in the late '80's, year or two before the first land rush to Oklahoma. There was a Texas rancher, name of Riley Cochran, raising longhorns down near San Antonio. Had a boy Billy about ten years old. Billy'd been raised in a saddle, you might say, and was stubborn-set to go on his father's next cattle drive to Abilene. The Boss was just as stubborn-set against it.

(*Stage lights dim, spot on far side of stage where* BILLY *and the* BOSS *enter.*)

BILLY: Lemme go, Pa.

BOSS: Billy, I've told you a hundred times I can't be bothered with a shorthorn like you when I'll have nigh to twenty-five hundred longhorns on my mind. You stay home and look after your mother.

BILLY: Chuck'll look after her. He's not hankering to go on the trail. I'll earn my keep, Pa!

BOSS: How? (*Male voice heard offstage singing mournfully: "Oh, Bury Me Not on the Lone Prairie."*)

BILLY: That's Spike. *He'll* tell you I'll earn my way. He's let me help round up strays twice lately. (*Calls*) Spike!

SPIKE (*Approaching, singing*):
"In a narrow grave just six by three;
Oh, bury me not on the lone prairie." (SPIKE *comes in.*)

BILLY (*Eagerly*): I *can* round up strays, can't I, Spike?

SPIKE: Sure thing you can, Billy. Howdy, boss. You being plagued for a job by a new cowhand?

BOSS: Looks that way. As if I haven't enough on my mind.

SPIKE: He's got the makings, boss. The real makings. In a few years maybe . . .

BILLY: But I want to go now . . . *now*. This very drive.

This very spring. (*Spot out, stage lights on, as the* Boss, Billy, *and* Spike *exit.*)

MILLIE: Did he go?

MAN: The Boss wouldn't give in . . . said the trail was no place for a ten-year-old . . . streams swollen with the spring rains and all, and dangerous to cross . . . and trail jumpers along the way itching to start a stampede so they could cut off some of the stock.

STEVE: Aw, Billy'd have made out.

MAN: And in addition, the discomfort . . . sun beating down on clear days and dust from all those hoofs rolling up in clouds. Cold rain on the bad days. You know what the song says. (*Sings "The Old Chisholm Trail."*)
"It's cloudy in the West, and it looks like rain,
The darn'd old slicker's in the wagon again."
  (*Refrain*)
"It began to storm and the rain began to fall,
And we thought, by grab, we're a-goin' to lose 'em all."
  (*Refrain*)
Cowboys were used to it, but a boy like Billy wasn't.

LARRY: He wouldn't mind it. Spike should have stood up for him, and offered to keep an eye on him.

MAN: Spike did. But the Boss still held out. All hands had their jobs, you know. Didn't have time to fool around with a kid. Riley Cochran was trail boss, Spike one of the point riders . . . (*Looks around*) Any of you know what a point rider was?

LARRY: To point something out along the way?

MAN: To *lead* the way. And line riders kept the cattle from spreading out, kept them massed along the trail. Drag riders . . . well, they had the worst of it, coming up at the rear, goading on the stragglers and eating dust all the way. Then there were the night-herders.

STEVE: Night-herders! I know about them. A night-herder had to ride around all night keeping the cows from straying off, keeping them lying down chewing their cuds. Cows got scared easily by coyotes yapping and wolves howling . . . and when they got scared enough they stampeded. But as long as they heard the night-rider whistling or singing, they felt safe. (*Swings his rope as he sings "The Night-Herding Song."*)

"Oh, slow up dogies, quit roving around,
You have wandered and trampled all over the ground;
Oh, graze along, dogies . . ." (*Etc.*)

OTHERS (*Joining in for second stanza*):
"I've circle-herded and night-herded too,
But to keep you together that's what I can't do . . ." (*Etc.*)

MAN: That was a job, night-herding was. Riding around a cud-chewing black mass of cattle for hours on end.

MILLIE: But what about Billy?

MAN: That's right . . . I was telling you about Billy. Well, the Boss wouldn't let him go. Set off without him.

STEVE: Aw. . . .

MAN: The first day of the drive everything went along fine. The second day likewise, except the Boss began to hear stories about trail jumpers being more active than usual. Spike picked up news at one ranch that two drag riders had been shot a few days before and a bunch of cattle cut out from the rear of a herd. The Boss told Spike he was double glad he hadn't let Billy come along.

The third night they reached a swollen stream late in the afternoon, and decided to camp on the bank and make the crossing in the morning, 'stead of trying to attempt it before dark. While the cows were settling down and the chuck wagon getting busy, Spike thought he'd best ride up and down the stream a ways to see that all was safe. He figured it was a likely place for outlaws to hide out, in the trees along the bank near a crossing.

He hadn't gone more than half a mile before he spied a horse tied in the bushes.

GIRLS: An outlaw?

BOYS: Trail jumpers?

MAN: Spike hid his horse as best he could and went ahead on foot, quiet as an Indian. He came upon a lone figure bending over a little fire. Something about that cowboy hat. . . . (*Stage lights down, spot up on side of stage where small figure bends over, back to audience.* SPIKE *tiptoes in, watches.*)

BILLY (*Singing mournfully*):
  "Oh bury me not on the lone prairie . . .

SPIKE: "These words came low and mournfully . . ."

BILLY (*Whirling around*): Spike!

SPIKE:
  "From the pallid lips of a youth who lay
  On his dying bed at the close of day . . ."
  (*Breaks off singing.*)
  Billy Cochran, where'd you come from?

BILLY: Been following, Spike. Scared to ride into camp just yet, though. Scared Pa'll send me back. Figured if I followed one more day, I'd be too far from home to be sent back alone, and he can't spare a hand to take me.

SPIKE: You're a rascal, Billy.

BILLY: You won't tell Pa?

SPIKE: Dunno what to do. How'd you make out nights, Billy? Weren't you scared, alone and all?

BILLY: I stayed the first night at a ranch, in the shed. Stayed with a herd outfit last night. Only a thousand longhorns. They're not far behind, ought to catch up in the morning by the time we cross. I'm not scared tonight, with you-all not far off.

SPIKE: You've reason to be scared, though. There're trail jumpers around, Billy. Mean ones. We heard just today of three more cowhands shot and cows stolen. That's five in a week. If those outlaws find out you're Riley Cochran's son, they'll nab you! Hold you for ransom. And you know what the ransom'll be?

BILLY: Longhorns.

SPIKE: And no telling how many.

BILLY: What'll I do, Spike?

TRAIL JUMPER (*Stepping up suddenly, pistol leveled*): You'll stay just where you are, both of you. That's what you'll do. And put your hands up. Nab the kid, Henry. I've got 'em covered. (2ND TRAIL JUMPER *steps up, makes a grab for* BILLY. BILLY *suddenly kicks revolver from his hand,* SPIKE *lunges at* 1ST TRAIL JUMPER. *Spot out as muffled shots from cap gun are heard offstage. Stage lights up.*)

LARRY: Gosh!

MILLIE: Deliver me from the Chisholm Trail.

STEVE: What happened next?

MAN: The outlaws skedaddled, afraid the sound of shooting would bring cowhands on the gallop. They were right. In a few minutes line men were on the spot. They found Billy penitent as a whipped pup . . . and Spike sitting on the ground rocking back and forth nursing his shoulder, singing one of his mournful songs to keep his mind off the pain . . .

(*Stage lights down, spot on* BILLY *and* SPIKE *at side of stage.* SPIKE *is singing, very mournfully indeed, "I Ride an Old Paint."*)

SPIKE:

"Oh, when I die, take my saddle from the wall,
   Put it on my pony, lead him out of his stall. . . ." (*Etc.*)

(*Two* LINE MEN *rush up.*)

1ST LINE MAN: What's happened, Spike? How'd *you* get here, Billy Cochran? (BILLY *hangs his head.*)

2ND LINE MAN: Let me ease off your shirt, Spike. (*Does so, looks at wound.* SPIKE *keeps up his mournful singing.*) That's a mean one. Think you can make it to camp? (*Helps* SPIKE *to his feet*)

SPIKE: You'd best come along, Billy, and face the music. (*To* LINE MEN) Trail jumpers. After the kid. (*Holds arm as he goes out singing "Oh Bury Me Not on the Lone Prairie." Spot out, stage lights up.*)

MILLIE: Golly! What'd the Boss do to Billy?

STEVE: Did the outlaws come again?

LARRY: What about Spike . . . was he hurt bad?

MORTON: Did the drive get to Abilene all right?

MAN: Wait a minute . . . one thing at a time. Billy? The Boss was pretty mad. Thought the best punishment would be to make Billy ride the drag, through all that dust churned up by the cattle day after day. Thought that would get a cattle drive out of his system.

MORTON: But I thought the drag was the most dangerous place . . . at the rear of the drive . . . where trail jumpers tried to cut off some of the herd!

MAN: Normally it *was* the most dangerous place. But, you see, that other herd of a thousand longhorns caught up with the Boss's herd at the crossing, so the two groups went on together. That meant more men on the drag . . . doubled the guard. Billy took his medicine. Yes, and the drive reached Abilene all right, only fifty or a hundred cows short, which was a good record for those days.

LARRY: And Spike?

MAN: That was a bad wound. Spike lost the use of his arm, pretty much. The Boss pensioned him off handsome . . . for what he'd done for Billy. A year or two later Spike got himself a good homestead in the Cherokee Strip of Oklahoma during the land rush of '89. He married and settled down, and I reckon he sang his mournful songs to the last. (*Background music from offstage—"Oh Bury Me Not on the Lone Prairie."*)

MORTON: That was a good story, sir. Did you make it up?

MAN: It's true as any story ever told. I was there.

BOYS *and* GIRLS: On the Old Chisholm Trail?

MAN: On the Old Chisholm Trail. You see, my name is William Riley Cochran . . . *Billy* Cochran. I was that ten-year-old Billy.

BOYS *and* GIRLS: Billy!

STEVE: Gosh!

MORTON: Did it work . . . the Boss's punishment? Did riding the drag get cattle drives out of your system?

MAN: No, it didn't. But, of course, there weren't many cattle drives after that . . . with the country settling up fast and railroads branching out and barbed wire fences going up. But I never got over wanting to be a cow man. I've a little old ranch out in Texas right now, where I raise a couple hundred head of shorthorns . . . fenced in. Came here for a week to visit my daughter and granddaughter, but—you know—I can't wait to get back home on the range. (*Begins to sing "Home on the Range"*) "Oh, give me a home, where the buffalo roam, Where the deer and the antelope play . . ." (*Etc.*)

BOYS *and* GIRLS (*Joining in*): "Where seldom is heard a discouraging word, And the skies are not cloudy all day . . ." (*Etc.*)

(*They sing at least three stanzas, all five if desired, before the curtain closes.*)

THE END

Songs of America Growing

Characters

FOUR GIRLS, *for quartette*

UNCLE SAM

ETHAN
HIS FATHER } *whaling scene*

COOKEE
LOUIE } *lumbering scene*

WAGONER
PIONEER WOMAN } *crossing Appalachians*

LYDIA ROOSEVELT
BETSY } *steamboat scene*

FOUR BOYS

COTTON PICKER

BOYS AND GIRLS, *representing different nations*

FOUR RAILROAD WORKERS

RAILROAD OFFICIAL

NEWSBOY

Note: Words and music to the songs in this program may be found in *Fireside Book of Folk Songs,* by Boni and Lloyd, Simon & Schuster, New York, 1947; *Fireside Book of Favorite American Songs,* by Boni and Lloyd, Simon & Schuster, New York, 1952; *A Treasury of American Songs,* by Downes and Seigmeister, Knopf, New York, 1943; *Singing Holidays,* by Oscar Brand, Knopf, New York, 1957. The words and music for "Sail, Sail Thy Best, Ship of Democracy," may be found in the March, 1957 issue of *NEA Journal* (pp. 192-193), or procured from Carl Fischer, Inc., 62 Cooper Square, New York 3, N. Y. (The music for this poem by Walt Whitman was written by Dr. Howard Hanson upon the request of the NEA Centennial Commission.)

TIME: *The present*

SETTING: *The stage is bare, except for a few seats for the quartette.*

AT RISE: GIRLS *of quartette are standing informally at one side of stage singing.*

GIRLS (*Singing the spiritual "He's Got the Whole World"*): "He's got the whole world in His hands . . ." (*Etc.*)
(UNCLE SAM *comes in during singing stands listening.*)
"He's got the wind and the rain in His hands,
He's got the sun and the moon in His hands,
He's got the wind and the rain in His hands,
He's got the whole world in His hands."

UNCLE SAM: Yes, He's got the whole world in His hands, the good Lord has . . . but He's given us Americans a good piece of it to look after for a while . . . to grow up with, you might say . . . to care for and develop . . . and pass along in good condition.

1ST GIRL: Why, it's Uncle Sam!

OTHERS: Uncle Sam!

UNCLE SAM: Surprised to see me, are you? Don't mind my poking around. Go on with your singing . . . I like listening. 'Tisn't often I have time for music nowadays, with so much on my mind. Always did enjoy hearing folks sing.

2ND GIRL: Is there any song you'd especially like to hear?

3RD GIRL: Or a choral reading or something?

UNCLE SAM: *You* make the choice. That's what I'm poking around for, you see . . . to hear what folks are saying and thinking . . . to get a bit of perspective on this country of ours. Don't mind me. (*Starts to look around again*) "He's got the whole world in His hands." I like that. Puts me in a mood to look at things from away off, and that's a good way to look at them now and again. (*Walks across stage*)

4TH GIRL: What shall it be?

1ST GIRL: What about that piece by Walt Whitman on America singing?

2ND GIRL: That's a good choice.

ALL GIRLS: "I hear America singing, the varied carols I hear,"

1ST GIRL: "Those of mechanics, each one singing his as it should be, blithe and strong,"

2ND GIRL: "The carpenter singing his as he measures his plank or beam,"

3RD GIRL: "The mason singing his as he makes ready for work, or leaves off work,"

4TH GIRL: "The boatman singing what belongs to him in his boat, the deckhand singing on the steamboat deck,"

1ST GIRL: "The shoemaker singing as he sits on his bench, the hatter singing as he stands,"

2ND GIRL: "The woodcutter's song,"

3RD GIRL: "The plowboy's on his way in the morning, or at noon intermission or at sundown,"

4TH GIRL: "The delicious singing of the mother, or of the young wife at work, or of the girl sewing or washing,"

ALL GIRLS: "Each singing what belongs to him or her and to none else,

The day what belongs to the day—at night the party of young fellows, robust, friendly,

Singing with open mouths their strong melodious songs."

(UNCLE SAM *has been listening reflectively.*)

UNCLE SAM: Thank you for that, for calling it to my mind again. I've been listening to America singing for a good many years as it's been growing up, but there's been so much going on lately, the "varied carols" Whitman was talking about have been crowded out.

3RD GIRL: How was it, Uncle Sam, when America was growing up, the way you say?

4TH GIRL: What did they sing back then when America was new?

UNCLE SAM: What did they sing back then? Well, let me see. Most of the early settlers went in for farming, you know, raising their own corn and beans. And farmers are independent folk. They don't sing together to do a job . . . mostly they work alone, clearing the land and plowing and sowing and gathering in the crop.

But the colonists weren't all men of the land, even back in the 1600's when the country was just starting out. Whaling and lumbering lured a goodly number of them, and they worked together, singing what belonged to them . . . singing of ships and forests, of sails and lumber camps.

Take whaling, now. New Bedford, Massachusetts, became the foremost whaling port in the world, with Nantucket Island running a close second.

GIRLS (*Swinging into "Blow, Ye Winds of the Morning"*):
" 'Tis advertised in Boston, New York and Buffalo,
Five hundred brave Americans a-whaling for to go.
Singing, blow, ye winds of the morning,
Blow, ye winds, high-ho!
Clear away your running gear
And blow, boys, blow!

"They send you to New Bedford, that famous whaling port,
And give you to some land-sharks to board and fit you out . . ." (*Etc.*)

UNCLE SAM: They sailed north and south and across the seven seas, those whalers did, while their womenfolk stayed home and waited and watched. Many an old square-rigger never made it home again, and many a gallant sailor went down to a watery grave. Yet there was hardly a lad in New England who did not yearn to join the whaling fleet. (*Spot on side of stage.* ETHAN *and* FATHER *come in talking.*)

FATHER: It's a hard and dangerous life, son. I don't want you to go.

ETHAN: *You* went.

FATHER: It's no life, I tell you. You'd be away from home for two to three years at a stretch. (*Shakes his head*)

ETHAN: But it's a chance to see what's off there beyond the horizon. Think of the excitement of being at sea . . . and sighting and chasing whales!

FATHER: And sloshing around on deck in a storm, with wind shrieking in the rigging and tearing the canvas to shreds. Yes, and don't forget that more than one boat has been smashed to bits by a wounded whale, son.

ETHAN: You get board and bunk all the time you're out. And it's a way to get ahead . . . divvying up the profits.

FATHER: A way to get ahead? Maybe it is, and maybe it isn't. Often enough there's precious little money left to divvy up after the expenses of a voyage are paid. And as for board and bunk . . . (*Shrugs*) you've never tasted whaler's "duff," I take it. Well, I have. 'Tis mostly no more than hardtack pounded up with molasses in a bag.

ETHAN: Still and all, it's whaling I want, Father. It's what I want to do . . . to be right there pushing on the capstan bar whilst hoisting anchor! (FATHER *shakes head, goes out.* ETHAN *sings "Yo, Heave, Ho!"*)

"Yo, heave, ho!
Round the capstan go,
Heave, men, with a will,
Tramp, and tramp it still!
The anchor must be weighed . . ." (*Etc.*)
(*He sings a stanza or two, then exits and the spot goes out.*)

UNCLE SAM: Eastward went the whaling ships from New Bedford and Nantucket, till they struck their course.

Westward went the bullwhackers with their ox teams, seeking the white pine.

GIRLS (*Swinging into "The Oxen Song"*):
"Come all you bold ox teamsters,
Wherever you may be,
I hope you'll pay attention
And listen unto me."

UNCLE SAM: They didn't let any grass grow under their feet, the lumbermen didn't. Early as 1623 they had a sawmill going, up in Maine. And before you could half-way turn around, they were shipping tall straight masts and ship spars back to England, and shingles and staves. Nobody'd ever seen anything like those white pine masts. Bowled the British over . . . masts a hundred and more feet long, all of a piece, and straight as a plumb line. Paid the colonists a hundred pounds each for them, the English did. Up to then they'd had to piece together their masts out of Riga fir.

Those days, the whole eastern part of the country was covered with virgin timber. Most of Pennsylvania and New York was one great white pine forest . . . trees running up to 150 feet and more, bare of branches more than half the way. It wasn't any wonder the lumbermen moved in.

GIRLS (*Singing second stanza of "The Oxen Song"*):
"It's of a bold ox teamster,
His name I'll tell to you,
His name was Johnny Carpenter,
He pulled the oxen through."

UNCLE SAM: The lumbermen moved in . . . bullwhackers with their ox teams, choppers with their double-edged axes, swampers to clear roads and trim off limbs, buckers to cut the logs. From the time the first mast was shipped to England, till the beginning of this century when the last stands of white pine were cut in Upper Michigan and Wisconsin, there wasn't any busier place than a lumber camp. (*Spot on side of stage.* LOUIE, *with clothes in a sack over his shoulder, comes in and looks around.* COOKEE *enters from other side and walks to* LOUIE.)

COOKEE: Hello. You the new man?

LOUIE: I've just come. My name's Louie. Canada-French.

COOKEE: You a sawyer, swamper, or bucker?

LOUIE: I make the trees fall. Chop, chop!

COOKEE: I'm the cookee. Help the cook.

LOUIE: Cook here good, boy?

COOKEE: Best in the country. (*Lowers voice*) But not to work for, though. He keeps me hopping, I can tell you, and he's got a temper. But he's *good.* Now, take for supper tonight. There's going to be . . . (*Enumerates on fingers*) thick pea soup, red horse in gravy . . .

LOUIE: Red horse? I never ate that in Canada.

COOKEE (*Laughing*): You've eaten it a hundred times. Red horse is roast beef, see? And there'll be boiled potatoes and rutabagas and windtimber . . .

LOUIE: That is a new one.

COOKEE: Windtimber new? It's old as the hills. Baked beans, Louie! The cook bakes 'em with salt pork, crisp and brown on top. Then there's bread and butter . . . and nobody can bake bread like the cook. And you'll top off with a quarter of apple pie or prune pie, and sugar cookies and coffee.

LOUIE: Sounds good. Makes a man chop.

COOKEE: I'll show you your bunk. There's only one left . . . you might as well put that turkey of yours (*Nods at sack of clothes*) on it. (*They turn to go out.* COOKEE *stops suddenly.*) Wait a minute. Can you sing?

LOUIE: Me sing? Not me.

COOKEE: Then you'd better learn. Look, Louie, if you

don't give 'em a song tonight in the bunkhouse, they'll toss you in a blanket. And let me tell you they can be rough. You won't like it.

LOUIE (*Shrugging*): If I sing they don't like it either.

COOKEE: Do you know "The Jam on Gerry's Rocks"?

LOUIE: I chop trees, not sing.

COOKEE: All right . . . if you want to get tossed in a blanket.

LOUIE: No! You teach me?

COOKEE: I'll be glad to try, before the cook yells for me. Now listen careful as you can. (*Begins to sing "The Jam on Gerry's Rocks."*)
"Come all ye jovial shanty boys,
Wherever you may be,
I hope you'll pay attention,
And listen unto me;
Concerning six brave shanty boys . . ." (*Etc.*)

LOUIE: You sing good.

COOKEE: Now you've got the tune, try the words along with me. "Come all ye jovial shanty boys . . ." (LOUIE *repeats, but he obviously has no singing voice.*) Try again. (*They do the first two lines.* COOKEE *sighs.*) Looks to me you're in for it. If you can't make good music, up you go in the blanket.

LOUIE: Good music? What about another way, eh? (*Takes mouth organ from pocket*) This way. (*Plays tune of "Gerry's Rocks"*)

COOKEE (*Pleased, nodding*): That's it! You play that mouth organ tonight, Louie, and you'll play yourself right into their hearts. Come on, I'll show you your bunk. (*They go out. The spot goes down.*)

UNCLE SAM: They cut down trees left and right for lumber for a growing nation—for houses and ships and mills and stores. They didn't think much of leaving something for generations to come. We were a young country then, and thoughtless . . . the future seemed a long way off.

Well, we kept stretching, reaching, bursting out of our bounds along the Atlantic seaboard. After the Revolution, folks started moving across the Appalachians in a big way, even though the roads were next to impassable and the mountain passes treacherous. Wagoners who knew the way made a business of hauling families and their belongings across the mountains to new lands on the other side.

They were a hardy lot, those wagoners. Had to face all kinds of weather, and be ready for washouts and landslides and mud, to say nothing of Indians and wild animals. But they sang out cheerfully as they plodded beside their oxen. . . . (WAGONER *comes in with long whip which he cracks as he sings, moving slowly across stage. Sings from "The Jolly Wagoner."*)

WAGONER: "When I first went a-wagoning, a-wagoning did go.

I filled my parents' hearts full of sorrow, grief and woe,

And many are the hardships that I have since gone through,

Sing wo, my lads, sing wo. . . ." (*Etc.*) (*He has just started to sing the second stanza when a* PIONEER WOMAN, *her skirt spattered with mud, comes running in, calling after him.*)

WOMAN: Oh, Mr. Wagoner! Mr. Wagoner! Our spinning wheel came untied and joggled off the back o' the wagon. Fell plumb in the mud, it did. My man's been tryin' to get it unmired . . . and now he's mired himself. We've both of us been yellin' for you to stop . . .

WAGONER: Sorry, ma'am. Couldn't hear a word of it. Where's the spinning wheel at? I'll see what I can do. (*They both start back.*)

WOMAN: How we're a-goin' to pry both of 'em out is more than I know.

WAGONER: Don't you worry. We'll get them out. (*They exit.*)

UNCLE SAM: Folks kept pressing westward . . . on foot, on horseback, by wagon; by barge and flatboat and keelboat down the Ohio River, and then . . . just before the War of 1812 . . . by steamboat. That was an exciting time in the fall of 1811 when Nicholas Roosevelt said he was going to try to take a steamboat from Pittsburgh to New Orleans—Nicholas Roosevelt, great-granduncle of Theodore Roosevelt, who became President of the United States.

GIRLS (*Singing chorus of "Down the River"*):
"Down the river, down the river,
Down the O-hi-o, hi-o.
Down the river, down the river,
Down the O-hi-o."

UNCLE SAM: Fulton had made a successful run on the Hudson four years before, but no steamboat had ever tried the Ohio or the Mississippi. Roosevelt's friends didn't think it could be done . . . and they raised a hue and cry when news leaked out that Mrs. Roosevelt intended to go along. (*Spot on side of stage.* LYDIA ROOSEVELT *and* BETSY, *a friend, come in talking earnestly.*)

BETSY: Lydia dear, you *must* change your mind. It's utter folly . . . utter madness.

LYDIA: Why is it folly? Mr. Fulton ran the *Clermont* from New York to Albany four years ago, and nothing terrible happened in all the five days he was gone.

BETSY: But you'll be away much longer. All those miles from Pittsburgh to New Orleans! You can't begin to do it in two weeks.

LYDIA: Nicholas thinks we can.

BETSY: And the uncertainty about currents and channel

depth and all . . . oh, Lydia, why endanger your life like this? Let your husband go if he must. He has no *right* to take you.

LYDIA: He's not taking me, Betsy. I'm going of my own free will . . . and looking forward to it, what's more.

BETSY: It's madness. For Mr. Fulton to test his steamboat on a well-known river like the Hudson was one thing. For your husband to try to take a boat down the Ohio and Mississippi is quite another. No steamboat has yet navigated the western waters.

LYDIA: That's just it . . . don't you see? That why it's so exciting. And, goodness, if anything's going to happen, I wouldn't want Nicholas to be alone. I'd want to be with him. Why, we're even taking our big dog. Besides, what could happen?

BETSY: What could happen! Steamboats blow up, and get stuck on snags and sandbars, and go to pieces on rapids. If your husband wants to throw his life away, that's up to him. He shouldn't be reckless with yours.

LYDIA: I have absolute confidence in Nicholas, Betsy. He's been building boats with paddlewheels since he was fifteen years old. Do you know the first one he built had wheels turned by hickory and whalebone springs which unwound a cord wrapped around the axles? And don't forget he's associated with Robert Fulton in this venture. Between them, they know more about steamboats than anyone in the United States.

BETSY: Oh, Lydia, you'll never get to New Orleans.

LYDIA: I'm not a bit worried, Betsy. We'll be so excited we'll probably spend the first night on deck watching the forests speed past at nine or ten miles an hour. Think of it!

BETSY: That's just it . . . I *have* been thinking of it. (*Spot out as* LYDIA *and* BETSY *exit.*)

UNCLE SAM:

"I hear America singing . .
The boatman singing what belongs to him in his boat,
the deckhand singing on the steamboat deck . . ."

GIRLS (*Singing from "Down the River"*):
"The channel is wide, the course it is set,
And someone is singing a song.
And don't we have a wonderful time
As we go floating along.

"Down the river, down the river,
Down the O-hi-o, hi-o. . . ." (*Etc.*)

1ST GIRL: And did Nicholas Roosevelt and his wife really get to New Orleans?

2ND GIRL: Without any trouble?

UNCLE SAM: They got there, all right . . . and in fourteen days, too. They had a few anxious moments because of low water at the falls near Louisville. Things looked bad, but Mrs. Roosevelt refused to leave the boat. The engineer put on full steam ahead, the safety valve on the boiler shrieked, and they skinned through without taking off more than a coat of paint.

GIRLS:
"Down the river, down the river,
Down the O-hi-o, hi-o . . ." (*Etc.*)

UNCLE SAM: A few years later another great artery of travel was opened when the Erie Canal was finished. The "big ditch" stretched 340 miles across the State of New York, connecting Albany with the Great Lakes. The population of Michigan and Ohio began to soar, now that they were so easy to get to by the Canal.

Yes, America kept growing and stretching—north, south, west. But not without growing pains. Nobody can say it was easy to transport a family through the wilderness, to clear a piece of land, and keep life going in a primitive cabin. It took a courageous breed of men and women. (*Takes paper from pocket*) I carry with me a piece an Englishman wrote about the people of the woods when he went to Illinois in 1817. Any time I get discouraged about our stamina, I take it out and read it. (*Feels for glasses*) Huh, left my glasses at the White House. (*To one of* GIRLS) Here, you read it.

3RD GIRL (*Taking paper, reading*): "These lonely settlers are poorly off. Their bread corn must be ground thirty miles off, requiring three days to carry to the mill and bring back the small horse-load of three bushels. Articles of family manufacture are very scanty, and what they purchase is of the meanest and excessively dear: yet they are friendly and willing to share their simple fare with you. To struggle with privations has now become the habit of their lives." (*Hands paper back to* UNCLE SAM.)

UNCLE SAM (*Pocketing paper*): Yes, they struggled with privations. For years they struggled with privations, but they took them in their stride. In spite of everything, they sang. All over the growing country they sang "The Turkey in the Straw," and "Weevily Wheat," and "Home, Sweet Home," and "Skip to My Lou," and "Old Dan Tucker," and a dozen other old favorites. They sang and danced to forget their hard times. (FOUR BOYS *come in to pair with* GIRLS *as they gaily sing and clap out one of the old play-party songs.*) Down on the southern plantations, the Negroes were singing a new kind of song as they worked in the fields or sat around the pine fire at night. The music was rich and the words haunting. They sang of their troubles and of their work . . . (*Spot on* COTTON PICKER *coming in singing "Pick a Bale O' Cotton," and acting it out.*)

COTTON PICKER:
"You got to jump down, turn around
Pick a bale o' cotton,

Got to jump down, turn around
To pick a bale a day . . ." (*Etc.*)
(*He sings several stanzas, then starts out.*)

UNCLE SAM: How they thought of words and music like that, goodness only knows. (COTTON PICKER *turns around.*)

COTTON PICKER: I know, sir.

UNCLE SAM: How?

COTTON PICKER: It's this way. (NOTE: *The following is adapted from a speech delivered in 1862.*) Pint o' salt and peck o' corn . . . that's slave rations. I do somethin' wrong an' my master calls me up and order me up and order me short rations . . . an' a hundred lash. My friends see it an' are sorry for me. When they come to the praise-meeting that night, they sing about it. Some's very good singers an' know how; an' they work it in—work it in, you know, till they get it right. That's the way! (*Nods as he goes out. Spot down.*)

UNCLE SAM: Yes, the slaves sang of their trouble and of their work, and of the Promised Land ahead. And they sang of Moses who stood up to Pharaoh, and of Joshua who made the walls of Jericho tumble down, for they saw the pattern of their own bondage in the stories of the Old Testament.

GIRLS (*Singing "Go Down, Moses"*):
"When Israel was in Egypt's land,
Let my people go!
Oppressed so hard they could not stand,
Let my people go!

"Go down, Moses,
'Way down in Egypt's land,
Tell old Pharaoh
To let my people go."
(*They sing second stanza if desired.*)

UNCLE SAM: We let them go during the Civil War, and

the country kept right on growing . . . didn't go to pieces, the way some folks predicted. The war set us back a bit, but not for long, with the Homestead Act offering free land, and immigrants pouring in by the thousands and hundreds of thousands . . . from Ireland . . . (GIRL *crosses the stage slowly, singing some Irish song, like "Cockles and Mussels."*) From Germany . . . (BOY *slowly crosses stage singing some German song, like "My Hat Has Three Corners."*) From Italy . . . (BOY *or* GIRL *crosses stage singing some Italian song, like "Tiritomba."*) From Scandinavia . . . (FARMER *crosses stage singing "Harvest Song" or some other Swedish, Danish, or Norwegian song.*) From Poland . . . (BOY *or* GIRL *crosses stage singing some Polish song, like "Out in the Forest."*) From Hungary . . . (BOY *crosses stage singing some Hungarian folk song like "Peter and Paul."* NOTE: *This section can be expanded if desired.*) We grew . . . how we grew in the nineteenth century! How we spread out. From three million people along the Atlantic coast when the first census was taken in 1790 . . . to seventy-five million from Atlantic to Pacific a hundred years later.

The railroads had a lot to do with opening up the West and giving us a chance to spread out. They started building in a small way in the East in the 1830's. That was the time of the great potato famine in Ireland, and Irish immigrants, fleeing the famine, did most of the work of building the roadbeds and laying the rails. They did a good job.

GIRLS (*Singing chorus of "Pat Works on the Railway"*):
"Fil-lee-me-oo-ree-i-ree-ay . . . (*Etc.*)
To work upon the railway."

UNCLE SAM: But the greatest boom came after the first transcontinental railroad was pushed through in 1869. Building that railroad gave the country an exciting time, I can tell you. The Union Pacific started from Nebraska, heading for California; the Central Pacific started from California and headed east to meet the Union Pacific . . . each road trying to see which could lay the most track. Chinese laborers worked frantically for the Central Pacific, Irish laborers for the Union Pacific, and as the two roads neared each other, twenty thousand men were on the job, laying two miles of track a day. (*Offstage at one side is heard rhythmic pounding as* RAILROAD WORKERS *sing the first stanza of "Take This Hammer." After a pause, pounding and singing are heard in wings on other side of stage, as other* WORKERS *sing second stanza of "Take This Hammer."*)

1ST GROUP OF WORKERS (*Offstage*):
  "Take this hammer, (Huh!)
  Carry it to the captain, (Huh!)
  Take this hammer, (Huh!)
  Carry it to the captain, (Huh!) . . ." (*Etc.*)

2ND GROUP OF WORKERS (*Offstage*):
  "If he asks you (Huh!)
  Was I running, (Huh!)
  If he asks you (Huh!)
  Was I running, (Huh!) . . ." (*Etc.*)

UNCLE SAM: In May of '69, the two roads were coming close to each other, near Ogden, Utah, with trains pushing up from behind. Telegraph lines were brought up, so when the final spike was hammered into place, the news could be sent straight off to telegraph offices across the country. (*Spot on two Irish* RAILROAD WORKERS, *as they come in driving spikes. One holds spike, the other pounds in rhythm as they keep singing "Take This Hammer." Two Chinese* RAILROAD WORKERS *enter from the other side and do likewise. Both pairs move toward center of stage. A* RAILROAD OFFICIAL *hurries in with spike wrapped in gold paper. There is offstage yelling and excitement as the* WORKERS *near each other. When they reach mid-stage,* OFFICIAL *hands one of the Irishmen his spike. Irishman holds spike while* OFFICIAL *gives it a weak pound with the hammer. The Irishman has to finish the job. Great shouting offstage. A* NEWSBOY *hurries in.*)

NEWSBOY: Extra! Extra! News just in over the telegraph! Last spike driven in transcontinental railroad. Extra! Atlantic and Pacific linked by rail. Extra! (*Hurries off.* OFFICIAL *hurries off in other direction.* WORKMEN *pick up their tools and exit slowly, singing "I've Been Working on the Railroad."*)

UNCLE SAM: Yes, we've always been a growing nation. After the railroad, automobiles began getting us places. After automobiles, planes. After planes . . . rockets? We keep moving along. But we have fifty states in the Union now, close to two hundred million people . . . and there's not much room to grow in any more . . .

1ST GIRL: But, Uncle Sam, there's more than one way to grow. It's not just crossing mountains like the Appalachians or the Rockies to a valley on the other side. It's not just filling up space on the ground.

UNCLE SAM: Thank you for saying that. I've been hoping I'd hear someone say that.

2ND GIRL: And we've got to keep growing or we'll go to seed. Isn't that what always happens?

UNCLE SAM: That's about the size of it. "He who moves not forward goes backward," you know.

3RD GIRL: Seems to me there are all kinds of ways to keep moving forward . . . in science and research . . .

4TH GIRL: In education and inventions . . .

1ST GIRL: In health and world relations . . .

2ND GIRL: In extending Democracy . . .

UNCLE SAM: Yes, yes. I can't ever think of America as a

nation standing still. I hear a new song for a new age, a new tune for words that are tried and true.

"Sail, sail thy best, ship of Democracy . . ."

GIRLS (*Singing*):

"Sail, sail thy best, ship of Democracy!
Of value is thy freight.
'Tis not the present only,
The past* is also stored in thee!"

THE END

---

* *Note:* In many graduation programs, the word "future" has been substituted for the word "past."

Production Notes

SING, AMERICA, SING

Characters: 9 male; 3 female; any number of females for Girls Chorus, plus 3 or 4 to be cotton pickers; any number of males to take part in the various groups needed.

Playing Time: 30 minutes.

Costumes: The Narrator and the Stagehand wear everyday clothing. The Girls Chorus should be dressed in white blouses and dark skirts. Consult illustrated editions of song books and history books for other costumes.

Properties: Signs reading New York, 1769; Chesapeake Bay, Sept., 1814; Boone's Farm, North Carolina, 1769; Any Town, U.S.A., Aug. 6, 1945. Coins; hats for the Sons of Liberty; pen and envelope for Francis Scott Key; sacks for Cotton Pickers; ropes for Cowboys; flags, horns, and possibly paper soldier caps and sunbonnets for the Chorus (as indicated in the text). Possible sound effects include train whistles, factory whistles, and a loudspeaker.

Setting: The stage may be bare or, if desired, there may be chairs along the back of the stage for the Chorus.

Lighting: No special effects.

SING THE SONGS OF FREEDOM

Characters: 13 male; 8 female; 2 male or female; as many extras as

desired. (Many parts may be doubled up.)

Playing Time: 30 minutes.

Costumes: The four boys and girls, master of ceremonies and chorus wear modern, everyday dress. All others are dressed in the fashion of the times which they represent.

Properties: Book, for first boy; sticks, for Jed; wood, for Aaron; leaves, for Hartley; newspaper, for Joseph Hopkinson; letter, for Samuel Francis Smith; Confederate flag, for Confederate boys; stars and stripes, for Union boys; paper, for Emma Lazarus.

Setting: The stage is bare, except for a reading stand, for the master of ceremonies, and chairs along rear stage for the chorus.

Lighting: No special effects.

SING THE SONGS OF PIONEERS

Characters: 20 male; 9 female; male and female extras. (Actors may take more than one part, and some male roles may be changed into female roles, if desired.)

Playing Time: 35 minutes.

Costumes: The Reader and the boy in the audience wear modern dress. The Pilgrims wear traditional costumes. The Continentals wear tattered uniforms. The rest of the characters may wear typical dress of the period—long skirts, long-sleeve blouses, and bonnets for the women, dark trousers and rough shirts for the men.

Properties: Book for Reader; hymn book for Pilgrims; rifle for Mordecai, churn for Nancy, doll for Mary, sewing for Mother; wooden wash tub for Sally, axe for Ben; two red ears of corn for play-party scene; paper for Dr. Pitts; coin for Forty-niner.

Setting: At one side of the stage are a few chairs, at the other side, a speaker's stand.

Lighting: A spotlight should be used in the various scenes, as indicated in the text.

SING THE SONG OF THANKSGIVING

Characters: 5 male; 6 female; 10 or more, male and female, for chorus.

Playing Time: 30 minutes.

Costumes: Pilgrim costumes for William Brewster, Edward Winslow, Elizabeth Winslow, Girl, Boy, William Bradford, and Susanna Winslow. Early nineteenth century dress for three Women.

Properties: Baskets of fruit, ears of corn, pumpkins, etc., for chorus; book, for first woman.

Setting: Stage is decorated simply to suggest the harvest season, with shocks of grain or corn at either side. Two rustic benches at left.

Lighting: No special effects.

SING THE SONGS OF CHRISTMAS

Characters: 23 male; 4 female; 7 male or female; 12 or more, male or female, for chorus. Most actors may take more than one part, if desired, or cast and chorus may be enlarged.

Playing Time: 35 minutes.

Costumes: Master of Ceremonies wears modern dress. Chorus wears modern dress or choral robes. Peasant, Woodcarvers, Jeanette, Isabella, and Children wear peasant's clothes; 1st Woodcarver also wears a brown cloak. Martin Luther wears dark trousers, a heavy coat, scarf, and gloves. Catherine Luther wears a blouse, shawl, and long, dark skirt. Luther's sons wear old-fashioned nightshirts; Luther's Daughter wears a nightgown. Shepherds wear brown robes and carry shepherds' crooks. Waits wear long, red-hooded capes. Indian braves wear simple Indian dress and headbands with one or two feathers; Indian chiefs wear elaborate feather headdresses. Isaac Watts wears an 18th century English costume. Joseph Mohr wears black priest's suit, black overcoat, and scarf. Franz Gruber wears early 19th century suit. Phillips Brooks and Lewis Redner wear American 19th century clothes; Brooks wears a heavy coat.

Properties: Sprigs of fir or small red paper bells, for chorus; wooden spoon for one chorus member; coins, for several chorus members; Indian headdress, for one chorus member; drums, for two or three chorus members; script, for Master of Ceremonies; wooden box and bundle of hay, for Peasant; figures of ox, ass, and 3 sheep, for 1st Woodcarver; figures of the Holy Family, for 2nd Woodcarver; figures of 3 kings and angels, for Apprentice Woodcarver; flashlight torches, for Jeanette, Isabella, and Children; fir tree and stand, for Martin Luther; string of white Christmas tree lights, for Catherine Luther; small lanterns, big hymnals, and leather purses, for Waits; bows and arrows, for Indian braves; fur pelts, for Indian chiefs; large Bible, for Isaac Watts; two pieces of paper, for Father Mohr and Phillips Brooks.

Setting: The stage should be decorated gaily for Christmas. There are exits at each side and at rear.

Lighting: No special effects.

SING THE SONGS OF LINCOLN

Characters: 10 male; 8 female; male and female extras to be dancers, band members, campaigners, actors, and members of the offstage chorus. (It is advisable to have two actors for the role of Lincoln, one to play young Abe, the other, Lincoln, the man.)

Playing Time: 50 minutes. (If a shorter production is desired, the play could be cut so that only the scenes dealing with Lincoln's youth are presented.)

Costumes: All the characters wear plain clothes of the period: overalls and work shirts for the men, long skirts, aprons and shawls for the women. As a candidate and as President, Lincoln should wear the familiar costume with battered stovepipe hat, black coat and trousers, etc. (As President, Lincoln wears a beard.) Hay should wear a suit. The actors may wear elaborate costumes. The band should wear uniforms if it appears onstage.

Properties: Mending for Nancy; buckskin bag for Sairy; pack for Tom; gun, paper, for Dennis; harmonica for Elizabeth; knitting for Sarah; placards, as indicated in the text, for campaigners; buckskin bag, harmonica, paper for Abe, wood.

Setting: The various scenes may take place on different parts of the stage, with a spotlight on the action while the rest of the stage is dark, or they may be presented as regular scenes with as many furnishings as desired. The scene in the Lincoln cabin may have a table, a bed built in one corner, some rough stools, a fireplace with wood piled near it, and a door at center. The scene in front of the cabin has a chopping block, logs, and a backdrop showing the cabin. The scene with Ann Rutledge may have a backdrop of trees. The farmhouse scene has a rocking chair for Sarah Bush Lincoln, the White House scene has a desk piled with papers and maps (the piano may be at the front of the auditorium).

Lighting: No special effects (unless a spotlight technique is used for scenes).

SING THE SONGS OF SPRINGTIME

Characters: 2 male; 4 female; 2 male or female; 11 or more male or female for Children and Maypole Dancers.

Playing Time: 20 minutes.

Costumes: Characters wear costumes which suggest their names: Spirit of Spring, April, Easter and Queen of the May wear flowing dresses; April Fool wears a jester's suit and cap, and Arbor Day wears green tights with cloth leaves sewn on it. Harbingers may wear tights. Children and Maypole Dancers wear spring dresses or shirts and slacks.

Properties: Garland, cane, May baskets, flowers, Maypole.

Setting: A meadow. The stage may be decorated with flowers, shrubs, etc.

Lighting: No special effects.

SING THE SONGS OF TRAVEL

Characters: 8 male; 3 female.

Playing Time: 15 minutes.

Costumes: Everyday modern dress. The Policeman wears a uniform.

Properties: Cardboard sign reading "Special Today!"; gong; sheets of music; bicycle with an extra seat and set of handlebars attached to it; electric train and tracks; sled mounted on skates; string of bells; broomstick horse; delivery boy's wagon filled with hay; rope.

Setting: A Travel Bureau booth stands at one side of the stage. A sign on the front of the booth reads: "Business as Usual—Make Your Travel Plans Here." There are some benches at the back of the stage.

Lighting: No special effects.

SING THE SONGS OF COWBOYS

Characters: 11 male; 1 female; as many male and female extras as desired.

Playing Time: 25 minutes.

Costumes: The Man wears a business suit. All other characters wear cowboy outfits.

Properties: Newspaper for man; lassos for boys and girls; guitar for Larry; pistols for Trail Jumpers.

Setting: The stage may be bare, except for a park bench at one side.

Lighting: The stage lights dim and a spot is used, as indicated in the text.

SONGS OF AMERICA GROWING

Characters: 17 male; 7 female; male and female extras.

Playing Time: 35 minutes.

Costumes: Uncle Sam wears his traditional costume. Costumes for the historical scenes may be simple: overalls and shirts for the men, long skirts and blouses for the women. The Railroad Official should be elegantly dressed. The singers from different nations may wear costumes suggesting the nation they represent.

Properties: Sack of clothes and mouth organ for Louie, long whip for Wagoner, paper for Uncle Sam, spikes and hammers for Railroad Workers, golden spike for Railroad Official.

Setting: A bare stage, except for a few seats for the quartette.

Lighting: A spot should be used in the various historical scenes, as indicated in the text.